W9-BPJ-886

# Family Business
# Succession:
## The Final Test
## of Greatness

### Second Edition

Craig E. Aronoff, Ph.D.,
Stephen L. McClure, Ph.D.
and John L. Ward, Ph.D.

Family Business Leadership Series, No.1

Family Enterprise Publishers
P.O. Box 4356
Marietta, GA 30061-4356
800-551-0633
www.efamilybusiness.com

ISSN: 1071-5010
ISBN: 0-891652-09-5

© 2003

# Family Business Leadership Series

**We believe that family businesses are special**, not only to the families that own and manage them but to our society and to the private enterprise system. Having worked and interacted with hundreds of family enterprises in the past twenty years, we offer the insights of that experience and the collected wisdom of the world's best and most successful family firms.

This volume is a part of a series offering practical guidance for family businesses seeking to manage the special challenges and opportunities confronting them.

To order additional copies, contact:
Family Enterprise Publishers
1220-B Kennestone Circle
Marietta, Georgia 30066
Tel: 1-800-551-0633
Web Site: www.efamilybusiness.com

Quantity discounts are available.

## Other volumes in the series include:

# *Contents*

# *Exhibits*

# I. *Introduction:*
# *The Final Test of Greatness*

Few challenges demand more of a business owner than passing on the family business to the next generation. Family members' lifelong hopes, dreams, ambitions, relationships, even personal struggles with mortality—all figure into managing succession.

**Yet managing succession is the task that is most critical to securing the future of private enterprise in the United States.** Rising competition, government regulation, taxes, and other problems notwithstanding, the **failure to plan and manage succession well is the greatest threat** to the survival of family business.

Hundreds of thousands of businesses across the nation are approaching the retirement or death of their founders or chief executives with no plans for succession or inadequate plans that will fail to produce the desired results. For those family firms with plans, many will fail because they mismanaged the succession planning process. No wonder less than one-third of family businesses survive into the second generation, and only about 13 percent make it into the third.

Business owners know the stakes are high. Ask any group of family business people at seminars around the country to name their **Number One** concern and the answer almost certainly will be **"succession."** Consider some of the issues they raise:

*"I don't think Dad is ever going to retire. What kind of a future does this leave for me?"*
— The son of a family business owner.

*"It's impossible for me to just let go of the company I've spent a lifetime building. And besides that, the next generation is not ready."*
— A family business founder.

*"I don't think I'm ever going to own any stock in the family business. Why should I continue to participate in it?"*
— A daughter of a family business CEO.

*"We have a succession plan; it was decided by my dad and his brother years ago. My brother and sister and our cousins don't like it, but we don't make the rules."*
— A third generation member of a family firm.

*"I don't know how I'm ever going to get along with my brothers and sisters in the business."*
— One of several children in a family business.

As professional advisors often say, "Family businesses have only three problems: Succession, succession, and succession."

1

### The Final Test of Greatness

Yet the process of succession offers rich opportunities for business-owning families. Not only is it a chance to make the most of family business assets, but it is also a way to perpetuate for new generations the special privileges and opportunities of ownership. **It is also a chance to preserve a lasting institution that will reflect the family's ideals and goals** long after the current leader is gone.

For most family business CEOs, planning for the continuity of the enterprise is the ultimate management challenge. The owner must safeguard the long-term health of the business, as well as prepare and install a successor. Other family members' roles in the business must be mapped out. If multiple siblings or cousins are involved, as they are in nearly half of all family businesses today, the headaches multiply in kind.

Plans must be laid to hold down estate taxes and ensure the CEO's post-retirement security. And finally, when the CEO is also the founder, it means letting go of the business he or she spent a lifetime building—often an incredibly painful emotional experience.

Perhaps most difficult of all, **a great succession is one that hardly anybody notices. It is a non-event,** an evolutionary process arising from careful planning and the artful management of expectations over a period of years. By the time the baton is finally passed, the word throughout the family and the business should be, "Oh, that's what everybody expected."

To execute a smooth succession, a leader must perform heroically on many levels, both professional and personal. As management expert Peter Drucker once observed, "The final test of greatness in a CEO is how well he chooses a successor and whether he can step aside and let his successor run the company."

### Plan—and Manage the Plan

This is the second edition of the first booklet in the **Family Business Leadership Series** published by Family Enterprise Publishers®. It reflects many more years' worth of knowledge gained in the study of family business since the first edition was published in 1992. The earlier edition, for example, concentrated on the *founder* of a business. This edition identifies succession management problems and solutions for any family business CEO, whether the business is in its first or second or third generation, or beyond. Whether you're the founder of the business or the third generation owner-manager or the CEO of a business in which only your branch of the family is active in

*This edition identifies succession management problems and solutions for any family business CEO, whether the business is in its first or second or third generation, or beyond.*

2

*Part of managing will mean recognizing when pieces of the original plan just don't work . . .*

management, the ideas put forth in this booklet should help you grapple with the issues of managing succession.

In addition to addressing the current CEO, we also open our arms wider to the successor generation with this edition. If you're a potential successor, you will find these pages useful in understanding what the senior generation is going through, how the succession process works, and how you can support it. You will also gain valuable insight into what goals must be met before the incumbent CEO can separate comfortably from the business.

Two other groups should find this book helpful: (1) other family members, and (2) key non-family employees. The transition of leadership from one generation to the next is often the source of uncertainty for individuals in either group. In the family, a spouse may be facing the retirement of the CEO and all the changes that brings. Other family members may worry about how the business will fare under new leadership. In the business, non-family executives may feel intense loyalty to the outgoing CEO and experience uneasiness or even resentment toward the successor. They may be concerned about their own job security once succession is complete. If you are a member of either group, this booklet should help ease your concerns and enable you to support and contribute to a well-managed succession process.

This revised edition of *Family Business Succession: A Final Test of Greatness* is significantly different in another way. In the previous edition, we concentrated on creating a succession *plan*. You will find in this new book that we focus not only on succession planning but more so on *managing* succession. Recent family business research and our own observations as family business consultants tell us that good succession management is like good strategic planning. CEOs find that the real value comes in *managing* the strategy of an organization, but they have to go through the strategic planning process first. Once they've done the planning, they understand the real challenge and greatest value comes from keeping it current and implementing it.

It's the same with succession planning: **managing succession is the most important part, but you can't get there until you go through the succession planning process.** Part of managing will mean recognizing when pieces of the original plan just don't work—a desired successor after an attempt, might not want the job, or may have to relinquish the role because of illness. There will be setbacks to almost any plan, but managing succession means preparing for them and, when you must,

*. . . but managing succession means preparing for them and, when you must, taking a different road to reach your destination.*

3

taking a different road to reach your destination.

Good strategic plan follow through requires tools for adjusting the plans and for realizing results. Follow through on succession plans benefit greatly from tools for:

1. Business governance —       A board of directors

2. Family education, —       Family meetings, family
   communication, governance       councils
   and involvement

3. Management/employment —       Well integrated succession
   education, communication plan
   and strategic plan and involvement

When these tools are in place and their priorities are in harmony, a family business has what it needs for succession management.

## Succession: A Definition

Narrowly speaking, succession means the transition of family business leadership and ownership from one generation to the next. Broadly speaking, however, **succession is a lifelong process of planning and management** that encompasses a wide range of steps aimed at ensuring the continuity of the business through the generations. It includes factors as diverse as exposing your children to the business at an early age, developing teamwork among sibling successors, preparing for your own financial security in retirement, and drawing up an estate plan. (See Exhibit 1)

If preparing for succession is so complex, how can you break it into manageable pieces? Most business owners begin by laying the groundwork for transferring responsibility, control and authority to the next generation. Suggestions on how to do that follow. You will also find information on choosing and grooming a successor, preparing the business and the family for succession, communicating the change to the family and the organization, and, perhaps most difficult of all, letting go gracefully.

We make an important assumption: that you and your family have already decided to keep the business in the family. We know this isn't a decision that can be taken lightly. It requires serious reflection and a strong commitment by the owner-manager and other family members.

We also assume that a successor candidate exists within the family, although succession should be given just as much careful attention in businesses where only non-family candidates are available. Most of the preparation steps are very similar as those for family successors.

EXHIBIT 1 ████████████████████████████████████

# *Planning for Business Continuity: A Checklist*

___ Develop children's values and and capabilities

___ Create lifelong financial security for parents

___ Finalize the family's mission statement

___ Finalize the owners' estate plan

___ Finalize the business' strategic plan

___ Select a successor

___ Plan successor's personal development

___ Assist other family members in mapping their career plan

___ Transfer ownership and control

___ Build a family team of owners

___ Write participation policy for family members

___ Retain non-family managers

___ Install outside directors

___ Prepare for retirement

___ Prepare contingency plan for succession in crisis

___ Develop a new management team

---

## The Rewards of Succession Planning

It was hardly a typical father-son argument. The setting was a gathering of family-business owners. The father, founder of a convenience-store chain, was debating with his successor.

"I owe more to my son than my son owes to me," the father told a listener.

"No, I owe more to you," the son said.

"What did I create all this for? You're the one who is going to sustain it and grow this legacy," the father said.

"But you're the one who has given me the opportunity," the son replied.

Many business owners hope to accomplish more with their businesses than just the survival of themselves and their families. **They desire a kind of immortality**—to create or preserve something significant and strong enough to endure beyond their lifetime.

Many of these leaders find that the succession process opens doors to that goal. It enables them to pass on to subsequent generations some of the rewards of entrepreneurship—the opportunity to build, to manage capital, to make good

*A well-managed succession brings fresh perspectives to management that can revitalize strategy.*

things happen in the community and to have a sense of control over one's destiny.

A family business that thrives through successive generations affords the family a special forum to express individual creativity. Family members can learn the value of shared decisionmaking and working toward common goals. Younger family members receive an education in commerce and enterprise stewardship they never could have obtained otherwise. Involvement of the family in succession builds family teamwork. All of this heightens the business owner's impact and magnifies the benefits of his or her years of hard work.

Good succession planning and succession management also enhances the value of the business by assuring that it retains the most talented potential successors. Too often, the best candidates flee the frustration of their succession prospects, seeking brighter opportunities elsewhere. Some families encourage this, maintaining the business so "the children who can't take care of themselves will have something to do." Over time, this practice destroys the integrity of the business.

The entrepreneurial energy of capable successors driving the enterprise built by their parents and grandparents can create a powerful business. A well-managed succession brings fresh perspectives to management that can revitalize strategy. Dennis Love was only 31 years old when his father, the founder and president of Printpack Inc., an Atlanta-based flexible packaging manufacturer, died suddenly of a heart attack in 1987. But Dennis was prepared. He had worked in the company on and off for 16 years and had earned degrees from Princeton and Harvard.

"There was a lot of support for Dennis within the company, he had a lot of experience, and it really made the most sense to have him take over," recalled Gay Love, his mother and chairperson of the board. He reorganized the company to encourage growth and pursued a strategy of acquisition, including taking the company global by acquiring two British firms. Since Dennis took charge, the company has grown from $175 million in sales to around $1 billion and from 1,000 employees to more than 4,000. Four of his five siblings now hold positions in the company.

### The Succession Conspiracy

Despite the rewards of planning and implementing succession, **many family business owners find it easier to live with ambiguity.** Who enjoys thinking about death or disability, making choices among children, and letting go of a powerful, prestigious, secure position for an uncertain future?

In what family business consultant and author Ivan Lansberg called "the succession conspiracy," everyone involved may conclude that it is in his or her best interests to avoid the issue altogether. Many business owners resist succession planning as prematurely focusing on one's death. As one-second generation owner of a Michigan based manufacturer put it following a planning session, "I got killed off again today." Doing it means admitting that you won't live forever—a step they feel diminishes them. Spouses aren't usually eager to bring up the subject of retirement or death. Children don't want to be considered greedy or pushy and they also may have difficulty facing the prospect of their parents' passing. Key managers resist rocking the boat. Disrupting their own relationships with the founder in favor of a new, untested boss is unappealing. Friends and advisors hesitate to raise the subject for fear of offending the owner or hurting feelings.

Our culture offers few helpful models of succession. Most heroes are thought of as "dying with their boots on" rather than stepping aside gracefully. Successful succession processes are gradual; quietly progressing with many realizing a transition has taken place only after it is complete. The lack of fanfare in quiet success pales dramatically with the hero worship in popular business media.

**Dodging the issue protects business owners from making the tough decisions** involved in a succession process. They tell themselves that by avoiding the issue, they are retaining key people in the business that might leave if a successor were named.

These leaders are kidding themselves. Avoiding the topic doesn't mean succession will never happen, and key people in the business know that. A lack of preparation for succession may actually drive them to another company where planning for the future is more solid. Like the many other people who depend on a healthy family business—family members, employees, suppliers, customers, and the community—key executives invariably respect the business owner's courage in preparing for a new generation of management. They hope for no less from a corporate leader. In this sense, **planning and managing succession form the cornerstone of stewardship.**

Nevertheless, some founders continue to avoid the issue in a kind of final, unconscious demand for the loyalty of all those who depend on the business: "how can you lack faith in me after all I have done for you? Just trust me." In the event of the untimely death or disability of the CEO, it becomes clear that he or she has unwittingly created a time bomb. The surviving owners or heirs may be disoriented and ill prepared for management. No plans have been laid. The whole family avoided all the sensitive issues of succession while Mom or Dad was alive.

Yet the **silence has not prevented each family member from forming his or her own private expectations** about dividends, compensation of management, family participation, and rights to ownership. If worse comes to worst, each soon hires a lawyer, the first step into a litigious quagmire that can destroy everything the parents built over a lifetime.

Leon Danco, a respected family business consultant, assesses the risk: "If you don't plan, you'll have the satisfaction of knowing that it's the lawyers four limousines back who will be settling your family's future."

Even in peaceful families, a poorly planned succession is costly. Key employees may leave if they lack confidence in the new CEO. Estate taxes will drain capital. If the business is sold, an absence of of consistent, strong management will reduce the price, eroding the assets that have taken a lifetime to build.

To be sure, planning and managing succession can be daunting. But it is doable and these pages will guide you through the endeavor.

# II. *The Pieces of the Succession Puzzle*

While venture capitalists are not always the best friends of family business, they have a useful rule of thumb: As soon as you get involved in any deal, start working on an exit strategy.

Thinking early about exit strategies is sensible—not only in capital planning, but for management and ownership succession as well. **The first night you sleep peacefully as a business owner satisfied that you have a viable company, is the signal to begin thinking about the continuity of the enterprise.** Second generation family business leaders in their forties need to begin thinking about succession even while the founder is still coming into work every day. The founder's retirement is too unpredictable to use it as a trigger for beginning the next round of succession planning.

We want to emphasize that it is the business leader's responsibility to initiate and oversee the succession process. As family business consultants, we have seen frustrated members of the second-generation take charge of the process themselves when their parents dawdled or resisted altogether. But when that happens, it's not a pretty sight and the results are often less than satisfactory. The stunned senior generation becomes aggrieved at the children, finding it incredulous that the children seem to be taking actions against their parents. The children experience guilt over actions that the parents perceive as betrayal. Everybody feels anger and the anger builds and builds. The anger plays out in the business and in the family, drawing in the involvement of employees and family spouses. This creates huge distractions from focused business management and good family relations.

When the younger generation moves ahead with succession planning, the process often stalls because the senior generation does not buy into the children's vision. Sometimes the members of the senior generation consciously abdicate their responsibility. They throw up their hands and tell the younger generation to come up with a succession plan. Before long, they discover that no progress is being made and they begin to realize that no progress will be made until the senior generation takes responsibility. Sometimes the younger family members do succeed in taking charge of succession, but the process becomes one of revolution, not the evolution that we recommend.

Succession just works better when the incumbent leader sees it as his or her responsibility and follows through with thoughtful and timely action.

This doesn't mean that if you're the CEO, you have to see to succession all

*Thinking early about exit strategies is sensible—not only in capital planning, but for management and ownership succession as well.*

*It is the business leader's responsibility to initiate and oversee the succession process.*

alone. That truly would be an impossible burden. Keep in mind that **succession is everybody's business.** A lot of people have a stake in it—successor candidates and other family members, shareholders, your board of directors, key non-family executives and so on.

You will need—and want—to share responsibility with them as appropriate and to benefit from their knowledge, wisdom, perspectives and if they are family members, their dreams and desires.

### The Planning Pieces

As they engage in the planning process, in addition to a succession plan, wise business-owning families make a contingency plan — one to see the business through a leadership crisis:

—**Contingency Planning.** A contingency plan is an emergency plan. It recognizes that the possibility of the unexpected death or disability of the CEO is a major threat to family businesses.

**Many owners install an outside board of directors or advisors as an "insurance policy" for their spouse or family,** to help with a transition to new leadership if necessary. Unlike key managers, lenders, professional advisors and others, outside directors have no vested interest in the outcome of emergency leadership succession. Their interest is in the welfare of the business and the family.

If a successor has been chosen, he or she may be forced to act like an entrepreneur, assuming leadership quickly and doing what is necessary to sustain the business. The counsel of an outside board can be invaluable.

Whatever the case, contingency plans for succession are a crucial safeguard against untimely forced sale or liquidation of the business.

We don't dwell on contingency planning in this book. However, you will find a guide to such emergency planning in Appendix A. Consider what the family and company will do if death or disability befalls the chosen successor. This doesn't occur often but it happens frequently enough to warrant consideration. The steps you will take are similar to those described in Appendix A.

—**Succession Planning.** While succession done well is a lifelong process, most of the work of preparing for the transfer of authority and control can be done in a period of 5 to 15 years. It's a good idea to allow yourself as much as 15 years to plan and execute a smooth transition. Most

*Contingency plans for succession are a crucial safeguard against untimely forced sale or liquidation of the business.*

10

owners begin thinking about succession in earnest at about 45 to 50 years of age, with plans to retire at about 60 to 65. Typically, when this phase is started, the children would be 25 or 30 years old, with their formal education and outside work experience behind them.

Beginning the succession process at this stage allows the 15 years necessary to make a choice among multiple candidates. It allows you the time to develop and groom potential successors and gives them ample opportunity to demonstrate their abilities. If you're moving toward passing the business on to a sibling partnership, it gives you time to help your children develop as an effective team. **A 15-year time frame also gives you the opportunity to make the best use of all the resources available to you, such as using talented non-family executives to mentor potential successors, enlisting board members' help in evaluating candidates, or creating a succession task force to assist in the planning and decision making.**

The third-generation CEO of one successful steel-distributing concern is preparing for succession even though, at 54, he is years from retirement. With five third-generation owners in the business and several of their children waiting in the wings, it isn't clear who will be candidates to succeed him.

The CEO has begun developing criteria for a successor, building an outside board, professionalizing management, and making other changes to smooth the transfer of power when the times comes. By the time succession actually takes place, the process will be well understood and the likelihood of conflict reduced.

Once a successor has been chosen, five years is usually enough to permit training and testing of the heir apparent and to execute a smooth leadership transition.

*Succession just works better when the incumbent leader sees it as his or her responsibility and follows through with thoughtful and timely action.*

### Five Pieces To Manage Well

The succession process calls for good management in five areas. We go into each in great detail over the next five chapters. So that you have a quick picture now, however, the pieces that must be managed well are these:

— **Preparing the CEO.** You, the business leader, will be letting go of a part of your life that has been very meaningful and rewarding. Succession is not complete until you give up control of the business and move on. A properly planned and executed retirement, however, can be a wonderful, creative adventure, with meaning and rewards of its own.

— **Preparing the Business.** The business will eventually need to get along without you and it is your job, as CEO, to see that it can. Leaving behind a self-sustaining organization is the epitome of stewardship. Once you've done it, give yourself a well-earned pat on the back.

— **Developing the Successor(s).** As a parent, you have been developing your successors since they were born, instilling values and skills and attitudes that prepare them for life. Now their development becomes more focused on preparing them for future roles in the business, including the top leadership position.

— **Preparing the Family.** Succession won't go smoothly unless the family supports it. The process benefits when family members can discuss openly how the business affects them and come to agreement on such issues as values and a family mission.

— **Preparing the Ownership Team.** It's very common for the senior generation to pass ownership of a business to a group of siblings or cousins. Where once there was just one owner now the business is shared among siblings. To safeguard the business, the siblings and cousins need education on effective ownership, business governance and teamwork.

*Leaving behind a self-sustaining organization is the epitome of stewardship.*

That's the over-all picture of what it takes to put a good succession together. Now let's take an in-depth look at managing those last five pieces.

# III. *The CEO's Personal Challenge: Preparing for a New Life*

The attitude of the family business leader is the single most important factor in any succession. But preparing for succession often brings an owner face-to-face with unexpected emotions and daunting personal obstacles.

If you are the incumbent CEO, **you must face the possibility of feeling rivalry with your successor. Seeing younger family members make their own mark on the business can be a bittersweet experience.** It is tough to resist taking credit for their accomplishments or feeling like a failure if successors do so well that they seem to outshine you.

You are forced to recognize that your successor is accomplishing things that are independent of you. It's a bit like watching your little girl ride off on a bicycle for the first time. You feel a certain sadness and discomfort. "She doesn't need me anymore!" But you feel pride at the same time—after all, she has to do it.

**You may also find it troubling that the next generation is creating a new system— one that is completely different from the system you were comfortable with.** If you are the founder of the business, you probably operated as "leader central." Your power was dominant; everybody came to you for direction. Now your son or daughter is relying more heavily on a management team and on outsiders on a board of directors to provide the accountability necessary to a strong management in a business that is growing increasingly complicated.

*If you're wise, you will recognize that your successors cannot run the business the way you ran it.*

Your co-president sons make decisions by consensus. Until they came along, there was only one decision-maker in the business and everybody knew who that was.

The family, because it too is now much larger and more complex, is initiating a family council and pressing for other governance structures. "We never needed such things before!" you say, feeling somewhat like you're in a foreign country.

At first you may protest the innovations. But if you're wise, you will recognize that your successors cannot run the business the way you ran it. Its growth and complexity and changing environment require different strategies and systems . . . and, they must do it their way.

### Creating a Separate Identity

As the outgoing CEO, you must begin to separate your personal identity from the business. This is especially hard for owners who have spent their lives viewing the business as an extension of themselves. "Without me, this company isn't worth anything," a CEO may think proudly. Or an owner starts to count the CEOs

*CEOs who lack other interests are the most likely to have trouble later, when succession is complete.*

he knows who retired and died soon after because their life's work was gone. CEOs who lack other interests, or whose parents had a brief or unhappy retirement, are the most likely to have trouble later, when succession is complete.

Now, perhaps for the first time, you must begin to consider questions like, What is the value of this business, apart from me? What is my value apart from the business? How can I communicate what I do to a new generation of management? How do I move functions to other people? How can I pass on my skills? How do I transfer my business relationships?

As if that weren't hard enough, the business owner must prepare to let go of power. He or she must confront mortality, in a real and compelling way.

Often CEOs stall on succession because they fear they and their spouses will not be financially secure in retirement.

One of a CEO's greatest fears is loss of power in the family. What happens if family members are in conflict or one of them is in need? Parents often feel that keeping control of the business and its purse strings provides them with extra strength in addressing potential family problems.

An owner can probably identify many "good" reasons not to let go of a business, but the temptation to do so should be resisted. What's needed, instead, is a new attitude—one that recognizes that passing on a solid business to an able heir is as great and admirable an accomplishment as building the business in the first place.

### A New Kind of Goal

Planning and implementing succession can be as creative and fun and challenging as launching and growing a business. The goal now is not to build the business but to successfully pass it on while at the same time shaping a satisfying, enjoyable future for yourself. Incumbent CEOs who channel their energy and enthusiasm to this new goal are far more likely to relish the succession process than if they dwell on a wish to continue running the business forever.

One of the CEO's first steps is to lay the foundation for the succession process. Long before succession takes place, the CEO should develop three plans: a strategic plan for the business, a personal financial plan, and an estate plan. (The family should also prepare a family mission statement reflecting its resolve to continue the enterprise as a family-owned operation. We discuss the family's role in detail in Chapter VI).

*The CEO should develop three plans: a strategic plan for the business, a personal financial plan, and an estate plan.*

14

Many business owners call on professional advisors or outside directors to help with these plans. Briefly, the strategic plan will help identify the qualities needed in the business's future leadership—the strategic mandate. Managing a more diverse work force, coping with an increasingly international economy, managing risk in volatile financial markets and keeping on top of fast-changing technology—all are abilities that may be even more helpful in the future. Advisors can also assist with the development of team-building skills and a sense of stewardship of family assets that are especially important for CEOs of family businesses beyond the first generation.

The personal financial and estate plans should safeguard assets from taxes and ensure the senior generations' security after retirement. Few thoughts are more unnerving to an entrepreneur than the idea of dependence on a business in the hands of an unproven successor. **Parents need a secure source of income, preferably separate from the business, to provide post-retirement comfort and confidence.** For full leadership and ownership succession to take place, the departing parents must believe themselves to be financially secure—as independent as possible of the business for the rest of their lives.

You'll want professional help in drawing up estate and financial plans and a good advisor can most likely suggest solutions you haven't thought of. An accountant showed the aspiring successor in one business how he could buy out his father and uncle by exchanging shares for debt. Repayment of the debt provided an income to the members of the older generation and enhanced their financial security. The arrangement also had the unexpected benefit of forcing the son to sharpen his management skills. "I have to pay my father and uncle a certain amount every year, and so I have to make sure I earn that amount. You watch the bottom line more closely," he said.

The parent-owners of a small suburban weekly newspaper chain outlined their personal financial plan as indicated below.

**EXHIBIT 2** ▰▰▰▰▰▰▰▰▰▰▰▰▰▰▰▰

## *One Couple's Plan for Personal Financial Security*

**Goals**
— Lifetime annual income of $200,000 per year
— Liquid asset "security blanket" of $1,000,000

**Means**
— Long-term lease on business real estate of $100,000 per year
— 8 percent annual income on $1,250,000 of liquid assets for $100,000 per year

**Plans for Amassing $1.25 Million Private Capital**
— Extra "bonus" compensation of $150,000 per year for four years
— After four years, sale of some stock back to the company for $625,000, which the business borrows from the bank

## Post-Retirement Activities

CEOs who enjoy the most success in passing on the business tend to begin exploring post-retirement endeavors as early as their late forties or early fifties. Many eagerly anticipate their successors' taking over so they can begin teaching, consulting, writing, building a charitable foundation, forming a new business, or getting involved in their community's cultural activities.

Some retired CEOs find a special role that keeps them in touch with the business but does not permit them to interfere. Once SC Johnson & Son (known for product lines like Raid and Windex) was passed on to the fifth generation, the late CEO Samuel C. Johnson could be seen in national television commercials, serving as a grandfatherly spokesman for the Racine, Wis., company.

Frank Cotter had to find a post-retirement passion twice. He had founded Cotter Farm Buildings, a commercial construction firm that specialized in buildings for livestock and crop storage. It became the largest business of its type in a seven-state area, and it provided careers for three of Frank's sons and a son-in-law. When Frank was ready to let go and turn over management of the still-growing business to the next generation, he decided to do what he liked best: manage a construction firm. It was fortunate for everyone involved that the business had long maintained a fledgling residential construction unit that mainly responded when a customer demanded that Cotter build a house.

Frank moved out of his old office and settled into his new office as president of Cotter Homes, just down the hallway. His reputation for integrity and his enthusiasm for his work occupied him to the point where the junior generation could no longer just walk into his office when they had a question. Frank made himself available for scheduled meetings and tried to help out when he could. But he was so busy that it sometimes frustrated his successors, who first thought Frank would meddle too much if he were in the same building. Much the opposite—they couldn't find him.

Several years later, looking back, the four younger owners agreed the arrangement couldn't have worked out better. They were very appreciative of how Frank had handled his transition. However, they did have to help him out of a jam once. Frank had become too successful with Cotter Homes and needed a successor for that venture. Fortunately, a young manager was right for the job and is now leading the residential construction unit.

Frank is now again doing something he loves: working with his church group to build homes for disadvantaged people.

As Frank's story demonstrates, **entrepreneurs who find a new focus for their energies are giving a great gift to their heirs: a clean and healthy break with the business** so that it can continue under the leadership of a new generation.

EXHIBIT 3 ▰▰▰▰▰▰▰▰▰▰▰▰▰▰▰▰▰▰▰▰▰▰▰▰

# *The CEO's "Letting-Go" Checklist*

Being able to answer yes to the following questions is essential to a good succession process:

— Am I committed to family succession? Is it a dream I deeply feel?

— Will my spouse and I be financially secure after retirement?

— Is there a strategic plan in place for the business?

— Have I chosen a successor and set a firm date to retire?

— Have my spouse and I completed our estate planning?

— Do I believe there is life after retirement? And have I identified an absorbing new challenge or interest to pursue?

— Am I willing to let others take new business risks?

— Am I comfortable with my successor's style of leadership and the fact that he or she will be introducing new systems into the business?

# IV. *Preparing Your Business for Succession*

As a CEO embarking on the early stages of succession, **your goal is to create an organization that can sustain itself even if you are not there.** The point, in succession, is to see a business be successful in the future while at the same time being independent of the outgoing leader.

One very useful way of determining how to make your business operate without your influence is to ask the question: "What would the business need to do to maximize its value to a buyer—one who has very little experience running it?" We know that a business valuable to a buyer is one that is relatively easy to step into and run with some assurance that it will be successful for years to come. So it is with successors. You want to leave your heir a business in as good a condition as it would need to be if you put it on the market and expected top dollar for it. Exhibit 4 will give you a good idea of how your business should look when you turn it over to your successor:

**EXHIBIT 4** ▰▰▰▰▰▰▰▰▰▰▰▰▰▰▰▰▰▰▰▰

## *What Buyers of Business Will Pay More For . . .*

1. Upward growth trend in sales and profits

2. Good location for now and the future

3. Attractive product in high demand now and in the future

4. Marketing program focused on defined market segments

5. Trained staff empowered to assume responsibility

6. Reliable financial statements and management reports, and good controls

7. Up-to-date facilities and equipment

8. Standard procedures and policies in place

9. No regulatory threats or potential litigation

### Begin with Strategy

Strategy of the business is important for two reasons: (1) You need to assess what will make the business successful in the future and what it needs in the way of development or change in order to accomplish such. (2) You need to be able to match the company's

*You want to leave your heir a business in as good a condition as it would need to be if you put it on the market and expected top dollar for it.*

strategy with the talents and abilities of the eventual successor.

Even if the business's future success depends primarily on maintenance, with few strategic changes, it will be important to establish this fact—because the next step is to determine what role the successor will play in the company's continued success.

Rarely is there the opportunity to replace an incumbent leader with a successor who can provide an identical contribution. CEOs are individuals with their own accompanying strengths and weaknesses, and the business generally gets developed around them. In one business, an owner with strong sales and customer relationship skills develops a sales-oriented culture and a sales-oriented strategy. Production management is subjugated to sales needs and learns to live with the situation. The successor, however, may be a creative inventor who is very active in the design and engineering of new products. The firm's competitive advantage may shift to depend on its exciting new products, with sales, marketing, and a strong administration built around them.

If the members of the key management team all retire about the same time, the business faces a different challenge. Shifts in the talents of those in senior positions will influence strategy and shifts in strategy that result from external forces—such as the arrival of big consolidated competitors—influence the selection of new senior talent.

What incumbent leaders must do is leave behind a healthy business that can be sustained by something other than clones of themselves. Even if the business strategy does not mirror the CEO, a family business with a single leader is often dependent on his or her decision making, constant problem solving and involvement in nearly every aspect of the organization. "How can I not be involved in a quote to a major new customer?" such a leader may ask. "We need the business and I have a personal obligation to each customer. My name is on the product."

As hard as it may be, however, the dominant CEO should withdraw from such intense involvement and concentrate on making the business ready to thrive under other leadership.

## Providing Strategic Direction

Business buyers pay for an organization that creates profits. They pay more for an organization that has the capacity to "throw-off a growing stream of profits." Do you focus on profitability? Or do you attempt to "break even higher and higher?"

*Do you have an accounting system that allows you honestly to determine profitability?* Can you determine which aspects of your business are more profitable and which are less?

*Do you discipline yourself and your organization to focus on that which adds the greatest value?*

These are among the business effectiveness issues that a leader must attend to if the successor is going to gain a healthy business. Goals, clearly communicated throughout the company, are the key. In fact, organizations are structures of goals. For example:

- **Financial goals:** sales, profits, return on investment, growth, etc.

- **Control goals:** costs, inventory turns, sales per square foot, sales per employee, shrinkage, etc.

- **Customer goals:** number of customers, quality of customers in terms of the amount they spend with your company, customer loyalty and satisfaction, etc.

- **Organizational goals:** a successor identified for every managerial position, employees cross-trained to handle more than one role, etc.

In a healthy company, employees understand the goals. Budgets are not seen as just an exercise or a game, and the budgeting process is pushed deep down in the organization. Managers and employees alike are able to translate goals into measurable actions—cutting costs or increasing sales. Rewards are connected to the achievement of these goals.

## Empowering Teamwork

A business that revolves around the constant involvement of the family business leader will be difficult to pass on. Getting a business to effectively rely on a team of managers is often the solution. That way, a successor can step in and become a team leader, rather than the one with all the answers.

Transforming the business owner's role from one of a dominant, single leader to that of team leader is hard enough. An equally significant challenge may be transforming the management group into a collaborative team. Managers' energies may need to be refocused on both joint and independent decision-making (instead of following the boss's orders), managing successfully with distributed authority, and keeping the owner feeling confident that everyone is on the same page and moving in the same direction.

Providing strategic direction, with goals and action initiatives, is a very powerful tool in this regard. It helps to mitigate what we see as a common mistake: giving distributed authority for making independent decisions without the direction to make good decisions. Establishing policy is also a good way to provide direction, and CEOs preparing for succession can greatly assist the process—with the help of the family, board, and key non-family leaders—by transforming their internal philosophies and rules for making decisions into broadly understood policies.

New skills are also needed when a group of managers who have been working one-on-one with the owner strives to become an interdependent team. Chaos results if the group members don't have an understanding of a new accountability to one another (rather than to just the owner) and the proficiencies to pull off the transformation effectively. **Consensus building, listening, negotiation, problem-solving, and conflict resolution are all important skills that the management team will need to rely upon when it shifts from an owner who**

**IS the business to a business that is self-sustaining.** If such skills are lacking, we strongly recommend that professionals be brought in or seminar/programs identified to provide the necessary training for all key managers, including successor candidates. It wouldn't hurt to include the incumbent CEO, either.

### Sharing Information

Finally, providing adequate information is vitally necessary for others to contribute to running the business. But such sharing, especially the sharing of financial information often presents a hurdle to the secretive business owner. Closely held businesses often have closely-held financial performance information. Nevertheless, if managers and others are going to be able to make good decisions without involving the owner every step of the way, they need good information, financial and otherwise.

*Being generous with information, paying attention to strategy, providing direction, and building teamwork all lessen a company's dependence on a family business leader.*

Everywhere we look, from repressive, centralized governments to cultural institutions, we find that failure accompanies repression and centralization. Those who centrally control information and restrict access by others hope to make themselves indispensable. But what they really do is weaken the institution. What happens if they are not there?

Success is not guaranteed by open information, but it is often an ingredient that enables others to contribute at crucial times when the central figure is not available to make a decision. Open information goes along with allowing open ideas, views, and reasoning too. Giving people information and inviting them to think and to use it to the benefit of a business opens the door for getting something back. They may come up with better ways of doing things.

Being generous with information, paying attention to strategy, providing direction, and building teamwork all lessen a company's dependence on a family business leader. Putting the company in the best condition you can is one of the essential tasks that you, as the CEO, must perform in preparing for a smooth succession.

# V. *Developing Effective Successors*

Here, we are referring to management succession. Later, in Chapter VII we address owner succession. A smooth succession won't happen unless there is a willing, competent and well-prepared successor or successor team. And it doesn't make sense to wait until your children are young adults to think about their development as successors. While the process will intensify when they reach adulthood, it actually must begin when they are very young.

The components that go into developing effective successors are these:

— Rearing children for family business leadership

— Attitude preparation for the successor candidate

— A personal development plan for the successor

— Leadership development for the successor

— What to do when the successor is a team

— A personal rationale for the successor

— The process of choosing a successor

Let's take a closer look at each of the major facets of preparing your company's future CEO.

## Rearing Children for Family Business Leadership

For many family business leaders, developing children into effective successors is more difficult than building or growing a business. Raising children is a taxing responsibility by itself. Add a business to the mix and it becomes even much more complex and challenging.

Parents lay the groundwork for succession while their children are small. The values taught then-hard work, saving, investing, sharing, integrity, persistence, stewardship, resilience, empathy, —help foster smooth succession as well as good family relationships. So do the skills young family members learn: communication, negotiation, settling disputes peacefully, planning, and so on.

The signals you send in talking about the business at home instill attitudes in your children that last a lifetime. Many family business heirs hear nothing but complaints when the business owner comes home from the plant or office. The suppliers sent the wrong order, the bank is demanding a quicker payback, two people quit, and customers aren't paying their bills on time.

"Sometimes I'd likc to chuck it all!" Dad grumbles. Then he turns to his son or daughter and promises, "some day this will all be yours!" No wonder the child shrinks in dismay.

If passing on the family business to your children is your hope, begin early to present a balanced perspective on the joys and sorrows of entrepreneurship. Talk about the rewards as well as the headaches.

**Make sure your children understand that a role in the family business is an option, not an obligation.** Talk about the business as a career opportunity, not moral duty. We have seen too many heirs take on the mantle of leadership because that was what Mom wanted or because that was what the family expected. When sons or daughters assume a successor role to fulfill their parents' dreams instead of their own, they'll be conflicted and perhaps unhappy the rest of their lives. That's not what you want for your child. Furthermore, it's not likely to be good for the business.

Children should not be led to believe early that the business is theirs, no matter what. On the other hand, there is no reason for the owner to deceive anyone about his or her hope that management and ownership will remain in the family.

"If at some point you become interested in the family business, you will be very welcome. But it's only one of your many options," parents might say to a son or daughter. "We will support and encourage you, whatever you decide."

One more thought. We like the philosophy of Carl "Terry" Plochman, III, the fourth generation president and CEO of Plochman, Inc., a Manteno, Ill, mustard producer: "Do the parents want to raise heirs, or do they want to raise great kids? If you focus on raising great kids instead of heirs, you might decrease the odds of family succession (they might go elsewhere), but you will increase the likelihood that any succession will be healthy because of your children's independence and maturity. If you focus on raising heirs, you might increase the odds that they enter the business, but put at risk the process they need to go through to be effective leaders. My bias is to focus on raising great kids."

### Attitude Preparation for the Successor Candidate

Too many heirs approach their role in the family business as one of entitlement or take the attitude that they should get to do what they want to do. "Why don't you set up a film-making subsidiary so I can run it?" they may ask Mom or Dad, even though the core company has nothing to do with movies.

Some heirs go into the family business for all the wrong reasons: for prestige, wealth, power, or a desire to win the parent's approval or to use the business to work out unresolved conflicts within the family. Some may fear they can't make it anywhere else.

The wise Terry Plochman says that succession planning begins with "developing self awareness," and he urges families to understand what the motivations are of children who want a key role in the family business. Some of the healthier motivations, he suggests, are: A desire by the younger generation to consciously take on the complex tensions of a family business; the possession of skills that match the company's future needs; a passion for the business, and "a deep love within the family that creates a desire to work together." When true motivations emerge, he observes, succession discussions become more "real" and alternatives open up that the family might not have considered before.

Some families nurture an effective attitude by conveying to the children while they are still small that they are expected to rise in life—and in the business—on the basis of merit. Such families may also establish a written employment policy that makes it clear to the children what conditions they must meet in order to join the business and aspire to leadership.

Potential successors should be encouraged early on to think of the future in terms of **making the greatest contribution**—not reaping the greatest possible benefits. This dispels the notion that entering the family business is a birthright, regardless of the talents or attitude of the recipient.

### A Personal Development Plan for the Successor

A program aimed at the personal development of potential successors should be initiated early. (See Exhibit 5) Such a program enables evaluation of their abilities and prepares the successor, once chosen, to move on to the next phase: leadership development.

**Potential successors should be encouraged while in their 20s to get three to five years of outside work experience**, preferably in a larger company. Maynard Sauder of Sauder Woodworking in Ohio explains, "our policy is that you must work somewhere else where your name doesn't mean anything and get one promotion—then you can apply." This fosters new skills; fresh ideas and self-confidence, making the candidate feel as though he or she is in the family business by choice and can contribute—not because he or she couldn't succeed elsewhere. Outside experience helps successors learn about the job market and their own market value. They also discover that "the grass isn't always greener" away from the family business.

Successor candidates should also be encouraged to develop skills complementary to those of the incumbent CEO or other family members in the business. If the boss dislikes recordkeeping, for instance, the successor might develop expertise in accounting and data processing. If other key family members love the production end of the business but dislike "people problems," the successor candidate might emphasize professional employee-development skills. This approach ensures that the next generation will contribute something new, and also can reduce the likelihood of conflict between the CEO and successor.

When a successor candidate enters the family business, he or she should be hired into an existing job vacancy—one for which the candidate is qualified. This helps determine pay and performance standards. It also allays resentment among employees who may doubt the successor's qualifications.

The successor should also have an opportunity to learn from a mentor outside the family—a valued and loyal employee, an outside director, a family friend or advisor, or a manager in a similar family-owned business.

The CEO or mentor should take pains to teach the successor the company's history, strategy, philosophy and culture, so the candidate can grasp the underlying principles that hold the enterprise together. Understanding the foundation of the business is crucial to the successor's future ability to bring about change.

Creative business families find a number of ways to bring along potential

25

successors. When Bev Kirby, the co-owner with her husband of Quaker Boy Call Company in Orchard Park, New York, wanted to prepare her son, Chris, for his future role, she encouraged him to attend an entrepreueurial leadership program at the University of Buffalo. Quaker Boy makes duck and turkey calls and other hunting-related products, and Chris had worked in the company since he was a boy.

Still in his middle 20s, Chris was the youngest of the 25 corporate executives in the five-month course. From these classmates, he learned that company managers in other fields had to deal with the same issues and struggles Quaker Boy faced. Chris was also assigned a mentor, a business owner who helped Chris identify and work on some of the problems at Quaker Boy. After the program, Chris proved his new worth to his parents. His father, Dick Kirby, saw him as an individual who could handle responsibility and make good decisions in every area of the company. He also saw that Chris had a strong work ethic and had earned the respect of other managers and employees. Chris was named president of Quaker Boy in 2000.

**EXHIBIT 5** ▰▰▰▰▰▰▰▰▰▰▰▰▰▰▰▰▰▰▰▰▰▰▰▰▰

## *Development Opportunities for Successor Candidates*

— Three-five years of work experience outside the family business

— Coaching by trusted mentors from outside the family and perhaps outside the business

— Outside exposure, such as visits to other companies or membership in peer groups like the Young Presidents' Organization

— Additional education, such as university executive programs or seminars offered by industry groups

— Team-building exercises, such as Outward Bound, a task force assignment, or joint travel with other managers

— Rotation of assignments and cross-training within the company

— Involvement in business processes (board meetings, strategic planning sessions, company socials and ceremonies, etc.)

— Exposure to company information flow

— Autonomous P & L responsibility

— Job assignments that offer the development of specific skills, such as sales, marketing, finance, manufacturing, etc.

### Leadership Development for the Successor

Once a probable successor is chosen, he or she should begin a more formal program of leadership development. Ideally, this happens as the candidate approaches 30 or 35 and the person in power nears the mid-50s. Succession planners should map out a career path through areas where the successor needs training—operations, marketing, strategy and so on. Or, if a career path involving a progression through one function of the business such as operations is pursued, planners should design special opportunities to gain training experience in other functions, (e.g. early involvement in strategic planning and special cross functional task force participation). Performance standards for the successor should be written and regular evaluations should be planned.

**The successor should have the opportunity to run a visible area of the business,** such as supervising a department or handling advertising. As the candidate gains experience, he or she usually receives greater responsibility, including running a profit center.

Successors should also be encouraged to learn useful skills and examine values outside the business. Many join peer groups of successors to share experiences and lend mutual support. The Executive Committee, (www.teconline.com) or the Young Presidents' Organization, a worldwide group of CEOs generally in their 30s and 40s (www.ypo. org), are two such organizations. Many college or university family business programs have successor roundtables that meet regularly. Other successors form informal support groups of their own, and still others look to other kinds of experiences to reinforce their leadership skills. At the urging of

*As successors move through the more formal part of their preparation for leadership, they should continue to be regularly evaluated and to receive coaching from mentors in needed areas.*

his godfather, Arthur Ochs Sulzberger Jr., the chairman of The New York Times Company, participated in Outward Bound (www.outwardbound.org) as a teenager and became a devotee of the program. It emphasizes collective decision making, confronting and overcoming fear, and identifying one's own unique personal power—skills that would serve him well as he rose to leadership in his family-controlled company.

As successors move through the more formal part of their preparation for leadership, they should continue to be regularly evaluated and to receive coaching from mentors in needed areas.

### When the Successor Is a Team

Some business-owning parents have two or three or four or more talented children, all passionate about the business and all in possession of senior management skills. That can be a curse if you're committed to having a single leader. But if you're comfortable with the notion of having shared leadership in the next generation, it can be a blessing—one that offers great benefits to the business and gives your children a unique opportunity to work together as a team of equals. It is rare and tends to occur only in sibling generations.

More parents face this prospect today than ever before. According to recent surveys, nearly 50 percent of all family businesses now employ multiple offspring, compared with 20 percent just a decade or two ago. **Traditions such as handing the business to the oldest son or barring women from the business have been quickly crumbling.**

Young people's interest in working in family businesses has been growing fast. Family values and relationships are stirring renewed popular interest. Many family businesses have professionalized management, increasing their appeal to younger family members. Diminished attractiveness of career opportunities in big corporations and in professions have speeded the trend.

With so many businesses eventually co-owned by several offspring, succession issues become even more complex. Despite the widespread conviction that a business needs a single leader, a surprising number of family businesses today are managed by multiple co-leaders. The J.M. Smucker Company, the Orrville, Ohio, company that brings us so many delicious jams and jellies, operates with two brothers who are co-chief executive officers.

Co-successors each need to be put through the same paces as any other candidates—attitude preparation, personal and leadership development programs, and so on. But they also must be schooled in teamwork and must be able to convince the family, the key non-family executives, and the board that they can be an effective unit. It's exceptionally important that members of successor teams learn the skills mentioned earlier—communication, negotiation and resolving conflicts. While co-leaders may share in the business' key decisions, they have separate roles that must be defined clearly to fit their own and one another's skills. In addition, they must also have procedures and regular routines to accommodate the coordination needed for their team.

### A Personal Rationale for the Successor

Successors in family businesses have a tough role. They often cannot fulfill their parent's expectations because they are not like their parent. Some have trouble making their own mark on the business. In *The Trust: The Private and Powerful Family Behind The New York Times,* authors Susan E. Tifft and Alex S. Jones show that it took years for Arthur Hays Sulzberger, the retired chairman, to put his stamp on the business—for two reasons: (1) Adolph Ochs, his predecessor, the acquirer of the *Times* in 1896 and the man most credited, early on, with its spectacular reputation, was an acknowledged legend; and (2) Sulzberger was not only in his predecessor's shadow, he was the son-in-law. He was not a

*Incumbent CEOs or other succession planners should try to help the successor develop a personal rationale for staying in the business.*

28

bloodline successor. That made it doubly difficult for him to establish his personality and authority on the company.

At some point most successors question their commitment to the family business. "What am I doing here?" they may wonder. "I'm smart. I had alternatives. Now I'm getting beat up by Dad (or my father-in-law or my aunt, or things aren't working as smoothly as I want, or the family is complaining about my treatment of them). What's the point?"

Incumbent CEOs or other succession planners should try to help the successor develop a personal rationale for staying in the business, asking such questions as: Why do you see this as an opportunity? Why is this work important to you? Encouraging the successor to answer these questions thoughtfully early in the succession process can be of tremendous help later, when the going gets tough. Sulzberger defined his own rationale by seeing himself as a steward—the person who would preserve an incredibly important, world-renowned institution not only for the family members that followed but for a public that depended on *The New York Times* for its diligent and objective reporting.

**Often successors experience, at some point, a feeling of loss of direction.** Although they have worked long and hard to earn responsibility and authority, a sense of mastery eludes them. "There seems to be one final step I'm missing, and Dad won't tell me what it is!" they complain.

True achievement can't be found by following a map drawn by others. Dr. David Livingstone, the famed Scottish explorer of Africa, received many offers of help in his work as a medical missionary from philanthropic groups. "Dr. Livingstone," one group wrote, "we have many good young men who would like to serve with you. Have you cut a road through the jungle so they can reach you?"

"If they're the kind of men who need a road through the jungle," Dr. Livingstone wrote back, "then I can't use them."

Often, the founder's message is similar. Once the successor assumes control of the business, Dad or Mom won't be there to make suggestions or give advice. Late in the succession process, the founder may begin to test the successor's ability to make decisions unaided—to carve his or her own path through the jungle.

If the successor meets all these challenges well, he or she is ready to begin the transition to leadership. (Some criteria for successor development are listed in Exhibit 6).

EXHIBIT 6 ██████████████████████████████████████

# *Checklist for Successor Development*

— Has the successor gained worthwhile experience outside the family business?

— Has a clear personal development plan been laid out for the successor?

— Is someone other than a parent teaching and mentoring the successor?

— Does the successor have an opportunity to make an independent and visible contribution to the business?

— Is the successor continuing to learn useful skills and values outside the business, as well as inside?

— Is the owner-manager or a mentor continually teaching the successor the business history, philosophy, and strategy?

— Does the successor have opportunities outside the business to exercise leadership and gain respect?

— Has the successor developed a personal rationale for working in the business, one that will provide a sense of purpose when times get tough?

— Does the successor spend time with other family business successors, sharing interests and concerns?

---

## The Process of Choosing a Successor

One of the biggest barriers to the succession process is the parents' reluctance to choose among their children.

"I don't want to face this issue because I'm going to lose either way," parents may think. "Even if I'm right in my selection, I lose. I would violate all family rules by picking one of my kids as a favorite, or as more intelligent, capable, powerful, or trusted."

When family businesses stick to a more traditional structure with a single CEO, it raises questions about how a choice should be made among multiple offspring.

A successor can be chosen in several ways. Some business owners bite the bullet and make a choice, either very early or after a period of competition. Others delegate the decision to a board of outside directors or to a management committee of family members. In a nearly ideal solution, still others manage to attain consensus among family members, directors, and key executives—and, sometimes, among the successor candidates themselves.

What are the pros and cons of these alternatives? Let's take a look.

—**Early Selection.** Some business owners choose among potential successors very early, often while the oldest children are still in their 20s. This method tends to work best in families whose offspring are very different in age or capability—

*Some founders allow candidates to compete over time.*

such as a family with a very able 28-year-old and a 17-year-old who is still inexperienced and untested.

Parents who choose early may want to reassure everyone that they intend the business to continue under family ownership. Parents are still young enough to heal any wounds inflicted by their choice. They also want to give other family members who weren't chosen time to pursue alternate career paths.

**An early choice reduces the risk that unexpected death or disability of the founder will leave the business drifting.** It also erases the possibility that deciding will become more difficult as the founder and the children grow older.

This method can eliminate talented younger children from the running too early, however. It forces selection of a CEO long before the future strategic needs of the business have become clear. It also requires parents to make tough choices and take difficult risks, causing hard feelings among some family members.

—**Competition over Time.** Some founders allow candidates to compete over time. This reduces the risk of making the wrong choice, and it allows time for the strategic needs of the business to influence the selection.

Unfortunately, this method sometimes becomes an excuse not to decide. It increases the risk that no successor will be chosen in time—that is, before the incumbent CEO's death or incapacity. And making a choice becomes more difficult as children grow older. Candidates may grow resentful as their positions shift over time. "It used to be clear that I was the logical candidate, but now it looks as though you're not going to pick anyone!" they may say. And as the owners approach retirement, their parental values or sense of family may grow more important to them, making a choice among their children even more difficult.

Adolph Ochs, the original patriarch of The New York Times Company clan could not choose between two obvious candidates: his son-in-law, Arthur Hays Sulzberger, and his beloved nephew and surrogate son, Julius Adler. Ochs at one time even became severely depressed over the prospect of having to make the choice. Each candidate thought the job would be his. But Ochs died without making a clear choice, and in his will, he stipulated that a trust be created, with three trustees: his daughter and only child, Iphigene; her husband, Arthur; and the nephew, Julius. The trust was to make the choice of successor. Iphigene held the deciding vote and what could she do but choose her husband? There were bitter feelings over the decision, particularly on the part of family members who supported Julius and resented the fact that someone who was not "blood" received the honor of succeeding Adolph Ochs.

*The founder may ask the company's board of directors to help design the selection process, create a succession plan, and oversee implementation.*

—**The Outside Board as Catalyst.** Many parents seek outside help with succession. The founder may ask the company's board of directors to help design the selection process, create a succession plan, and oversee implementation. Directors can also help prepare and counsel family members involved in the process.

Some family businesses actually assemble an active board of outside directors or advisors for the first time primarily to help with succession. Ideally, the board is composed of respected peers of the CEO who can act as a sounding board and help mentor the successor. Directors can be an invaluable source of stability and cohesiveness at difficult times in the succession process.

*Directors can be an invaluable source of stability and cohesiveness at difficult times in the succession process.*

Business owners have to be wary of misusing a board, however. If a board is ostensibly given the role of making the choice of successor but the incumbent CEO, behind the scenes, is retaining the final decision, the family will see through the scheme and the board will lose credibility in the eyes of family members. It's also a mistake to create a board to assist with the succession process when the CEO or the family is not really ready for a board—not prepared to share information openly with directors, for example, or to truly welcome their advice.

—**The Family Executive Team.** Some parents assign responsibility for succession to an executive committee or task force of siblings in the business. This removes the burden of a decision from parents and encourages consensus among brothers and sisters. As this group works together, an obvious leader sometimes emerges. "It's clear that Mary has the ability and the wisdom to do this job. She also inspires trust and shows the greatest skill in bringing people together," family members may conclude.

This method can end in stalemate, though. It also risks encouraging politicking and the formation of emotional alliances that can hurt the business and the family.

Another possibility is that the siblings will decide not to decide on one individual, but to take on leadership of the business as a team. The notion of a sibling partnership may clash with the views of the incumbent CEO and others that a business should be run as a hierarchy with a single head. It also means that the leadership of the business is no stronger than the consensus of the siblings on the management team.

Once responsibility has been given to a sibling task force, however, it is difficult to override the group's decision.

—**The Non-Family CEO.** Some business owners name a non-family CEO and ask that person to pick his or her own successor. This method removes the burden of choice from the parents and can be used to fill a management gap if the business owner retires before any family successors are ready.

There is risk to this method, however, especially if the non-family CEO has sole responsibility. Non-family executives can be even more vulnerable to family politicking and worries about showing favoritism than family executives. They may fear a stockholder revolt. They also may lack the understanding of the business's values, history and culture that is necessary to guide their choice of the next successor. A non-family executive in this situation is especially in need of support and oversight by an outside board.

—**The Professional Advisor.** Some family businesses leave the choice to a paid advisor, such as a lawyer, an industrial psychologist, or a family business consultant. This method has many of the same risks as asking a non-family CEO to make the decision. Also, it is typically used after the founder has died—far too late for planning and preparation.

—**Selection by Default.** Some parents let time pass until most of the successor candidates have left the business for greener pastures. This makes the choice obvious. "The person who has waited the longest deserves the job," these owners reason.

Unfortunately, this method tends to chase away the most ambitious, eager, and talented candidates, leaving the least qualified prospect to take the helm. Also, there is no guarantee that retirement, death, or disability of the incumbent leader won't occur before there is only one potential successor left in the business.

—**Consensus Among Family, Board, and Executives.** Ideally, the business owner, family members, directors, and the executive team can agree on criteria, a selection process and a timetable for succession. Once this is achieved, a leading candidate tends to emerge over time with a minimum of conflict. Either the board or the family executive team can then act as a catalyst for a final decision.

**This process of "evolutionary self-revelation" makes a well-executed family business succession neither random nor choreographed.** The people involved are governed by certain principles or procedures—that a successor will be chosen within five years, for instance, and then only by consensus of the board and key family members. But no one knows as the process begins who will be selected. Instead, the choice becomes apparent over time. "Charlie has won the most respect of family members and employees," family and board members may agree. Or, "Serena's success at moving her profit center into new areas shows that she is the best leader." This approach can unburden parents and lead to deliberate, well-reasoned choices with less room for rancor within the family.

*Some parents assign responsibility for succession to an executive committee or task force of siblings in the business.*

—**The Succession Task Force.** Larger, older companies with formal boards and organized family councils sometimes create a succession task force to execute a more formal version of the consensus method described above. Key managers, family members amI directors make up the task force. The group may decide on a succession plan and a selection process, then monitor its implementation. Such a task force can also help with other aspects of succession, including compensation of key family and non-family managers, job descriptions, and team building.

While small to medium-sized family businesses typically use less formal methods, companies in the third generation of family management or beyond often use an outside board or succession task force to select a successor.

—**No Logical Candidate.** In some family businesses, it becomes clear during the preparation or planning process that no logical successor candidate exists within the family. An outside board of directors or a professional advisor can be helpful to the family in weighing its alternatives.

**At some point, all owners should at least consider alternatives to family succession, including naming a non-family successor.** This guards against the possibility that none of the children will work out as successors, or that all might decide to pursue other interests. Some families use non-family CEOs to bridge their children's generation, hoping that business leadership will be restored to the family once the grandchildren grow up.

Obviously, **we favor a consensus method of choosing a successor, particularly one in which the incumbent CEO, family members, board, and executive team agree on the selection process and support the final decision.** Whatever method is used, you need the most capable successor you can find. There may be dissatisfaction with the selection in some quarters. But the grumbling can't go on too long when a successor leads the company to new heights, assuring its continued benefits to family members and giving them new reasons to be proud that they are part of a business-owning family.

# VI. *Preparing the Family for a Successful Transition*

Business families have found that even when succession is not a current issue—but most certainly when it is—a means of productively involving the broader family is critical.

One business owner put it this way, "When we don't provide a place for family members to work out their problems, they do it wherever they happen to be. Too often it's while they're at work, with an audience of confused employees and customers."

**A forum in which family members can address how the business impacts them as a family and how they as a family influence the business has been found to be one of the most powerful ingredients available to a successful generational transition.** Family forums, often called family meetings or family councils, are useful in resolving family differences and problems away from the business. More important, they can help to nurture family cohesion and support as a business passes from one generation to the next.

Creating a family forum can do much more than facilitate a smooth transition. The family and business benefit in many ways. Communication improves throughout both family and business. Management gains confidence because it recognizes that the family backs its goals and efforts. Spouses gain an understanding of the business, and children profit from learning about their legacy. Even grandchildren benefit when they see family members coming together to work out problems and set the stage for the future. It provides young people with a valuable example of how family members can manage differences while retaining their love and respect for one another.

A forum provides a place for the family to educate and develop younger family members for their future roles as owners and leaders of the business. It also helps family members maintain unity and trust in the face of new challenges that come with the growth in size and complexity of both the family and the business.

Although there are many variations, we have found three types of family forums to be beneficial before, during and after succession; (1) regular family meetings, held to discuss issues of the moment; (2) a more formal family council, which holds not only regular meetings but also arranges educational sessions for family members and takes on other responsibilities; and (3) a successor forum, where members of the next generation can discuss their concerns and gain information.

Lindauer River Ranch in Northern California is an agricultural business with active and inactive shareholders in the first, second and third generations. They have a family council that meets twice per year and includes all ten adult family members (including spouses). Usually a month prior to each family council meeting and a few more times in between, the five members of the third generation meet as a successor forum.

At one point in time, the successor forum was grappling with the challenge of how they will manage the business with mostly inactive ownership. The question of, "What if we don't like the manager's performance and the Board isn't doing anyting about it . . . what do we do?" This led to a presentation at the family council on how they would deal with this specific issue. At the same meeting, the family council also dealt with a draft of an emergency succession plan in case a tragedy occurred to a current second-generation business leader. Some of this is relevant to the board of directors role, i.e. the emergency succession plan, but at the same time, the directors were mostly dealing with strategic issues of international competition, local market pressures, crop strategies and capital investment needed for environmental initiatives.

You will find an example of one family's Family Council Charter in Appendix B. Other volumes of the Family Business Leadership Series provide through discussions on organizing a business-owning family. You will find those titles listed in the Further References section of this book.

### The Family's Resolve

**A crucial factor in the outcome of any succession effort is the resolve to continue the business as a family-owned enterprise.** And that's why a family forum of some kind is so important—it is the arena in which the family's commitment can emerge.

One of the most important tasks a family forum addresses is **a family mission statement that articulates the family's commitment and the reasons behind it.** It also describes other aspects of the family's vision for the business and the family role in it. Some family mission statements are brief, contained in a few succinct sentences or paragraphs. Others may continue for several pages, including, among other things:

— A statement of family values as they relate to the business
— Policies on family participation in the business
— Principles guiding family-member compensation
— A family code of conduct as it relates to the business
— Policies on sharing financial information
— Guidelines for forming a family organization

Exhibit 7 offers an example of one mission statement, and in Appendix C, you will find an outline of questions that your family can use as you develop your own mission statement.

**EXHIBIT 7** ▮▮▮▮▮▮▮▮▮▮▮▮▮▮▮▮▮▮▮▮▮▮▮▮▮▮▮▮▮▮▮

## *A Family Mission Statement*

We are fortunate to have a privately owned business in our family. The business provides family members opportunities that are difficult to replicate: opportunities to earn financial independence, to learn the skills of business and leadership, to contribute actively to others in the community, and to share in common family interests. To work productively is to grow, to respect humility, to know the realities of life. Not to work is an unhealthy state. Maintaining the business in the family and seeking to expand and strengthen the business will help assure that our family will have productive work rather than live off the accomplishments of past generations. We are committed to the long-term success of our family business for the benefit of our future generations.

The business must be run as a business. In that way, family members will know that they have earned their personal successes; those who work for us will know that their careers and families will be secure. It is not easy to run a family business like a business. Family members will inevitably have needs and turn to the business to fill them. For that reason, we, as a family, have all openly pledged to help one another, when one is in need, from our personal resources—not from those of the business. We have provided an estate apart from the business to assure some comfort and security for each family member; we hope family members will forever prolong the prudence our family has always practiced by saving these funds rather than spending them.

All family members are welcome in the business. We are fortunate to be a large enough business to have ample opportunities. As in the past, however, family members may be asked to withdraw if their contributions and business circumstances so require.

We hope one or more family members will qualify to be able future leaders of the business. For our business, that will require excellent skills and excellent educational backgrounds. We wish a family member to serve as chief executive and to assume the traditions of our business and family, as well as ensure by example that it remains a working business for the family—not a passive investment.

To help ensure that the family acts as one and works hard to formulate common plans and ideals, we have established a voting trust. Three members of the family will be elected as trustees for three-year-terms—one each year. No family member may serve as trustee for more than two consecutive terms. The trust will represent the family shareholders.

Business decisions will be aided by a board of directors comprised of the three trustees and four others who are neither family members nor employees. If we are to run ourselves like a business, we should be able to convince the outside directors of the rightness of our business plans and goals.

The trustees will also accept informal roles as family leaders. In that respect, they will be available to help any family members in need or to counsel family members on matters of financial orientation. The trustees will help identify investment opportunities for all family members to share in (voluntarily). These non-family businesses investments will provide one form of common family interests.

Individual family members may suggest any agenda item to the trustees on a confidential basis. The trustees will make every effort to examine and resolve family differences.

In the end, this plan is no stronger than the will and love of the entire family. Together we can provide great opportunities for ourselves and our children and even their children. It has been done before. Surely we can do it now. Why not?

*Creating Effective Boards for Private Enterprises: Meeting the Challenges of Continuity and Competition* by John L. Ward, Ph.D.

---

When family members join together to create a mission statement that pledges their commitment to continuity of the business in the family, they strengthen and facilitate the succession process. Their action signals to all involved that they intend to preserve the family business as a family business for generations to come.

# VII. *Preparing the Responsible Owner Team*

If you are among the increasing number of owners intending to transfer your business assets to multiple heirs, you need to give thorough attention to the role of your children as business partners. Often, family business leaders are so distracted by the complexities of estate planning, personal financial planning and leadership succession that they overlook the issues presented by team ownership.

**Teams of family shareholders add value to a business when members are working well together as owners. However, disaster can result—and often does—when they are not.**

*The key is preparing your children not only for leadership succession but also for ownership succession.*

The key is preparing your children not only for leadership succession but also for ownership succession. Although these two aspects of succession are often very much intertwined, they also need to be considered separately.

There are a variety of ownership scenarios in the sibling generation alone. A few examples:

— Ownership is passed equally to all the children, all of whom work in the business as a co-successor team.

— Ownership is passed to all the children, all of whom work in the business. One of the children is CEO, while the others hold lesser senior positions. The CEO receives 51 percent of the stock because the parents believe a CEO should have control. The siblings become minority shareholders.

— Ownership is passed only to the children who work in the business. (If the parents are wise, they provide legacies of equal worth to the other children from assets outside the business.)

— Ownership is passed equally to all children, whether or not they work in the business.

— Ownership is passed equally to all the children but none of them work in the business. Instead, it is run by a non-family CEO or perhaps a non-owning in-law.

— Ownership is left by a grandparent to the grandchildren in equal or unequal amounts. The second-generation parents are faced with preparing the third generation members for their legacy.

You know how complicated ownership arrangements can be and how differences among owners can mire a business in trouble. Remember the sorrowful story of the Binghams of Louisville, Kentucky? The family had built a nationally renowned media empire that was worth well over $400 million in 1986 when the family completely collapsed and the business was sold. The reasons for the Binghams' failure to continue as a business-owning family are complex, but a significant factor was the extreme discontent of one of the third-generation siblings, a minority owner who threatened to sell her shares if the family would not redeem them at a price she felt fair.

Consider the concerns of a couple we'll call John and Lucy Burns, who own a hotel and restaurant business. Two of their children hold key jobs in the business, while the other two are clearly never going to join. One has become a physician and the other is a homemaker. John and Lucy are distributing their stock in the business equally among the children. However, they worry about how the two working in the business will get along with their outside shareholding brother and sister. John and Lucy want the four children to continue their family ties after the parents are no longer around to keep the family together. The senior Burns also hope that the business will continue to flourish as a family business, one that can be passed on to their grandchildren.

Perhaps you have concerns that are similar to those of John and Lucy Burns. You have probably heard stories about family businesses that missed opportunities because one or more of the owning partners didn't understand or support an agreed-upon strategy. You may know of a business that fell victim to the classic conflict between shareholders working in the business who want to reinvest profits in it and those not working in the business who want liquidity and/or current income.

Without consideration of the strength of the team of owners in planning succession, families may set in motion the destruction of the family and the business. Alternatively, families in which members begin early to understand their roles as shareholders can become a force behind a key competitive advantage of a family business: patient capital. Unencumbered by the demands of Wall Street for quick returns, a privately held family business can make decisions or take action when it is most advantageous for the company. The time frame may be short in some cases, but often it takes years, and the business needs the patience of a supportive ownership behind it to reach long-term goals.

For our purposes here, let it suffice to say that parents need to begin early to mentor heirs on what it means to be a responsible owner. **By their own example, parents can demonstrate the selflessness that good ownership often requires,** and they can see to it that their successors are educated on such topics as:

— The roles and responsibilities of the board, shareholders, and management.

— How business strategy impacts individual shareholders—and vice versa.

— What stewardship means in a family business.

— How to read financial statements.

Parents can also set an example for and educate their children about the kinds of decisions they will have to make as an ownership team. They will need to work together to answer such questions as:

— What does ownership mean to us—a stewardship responsibility or a financial investment?

— What guidelines should we follow regarding re-investing in the firm?

— What mechanisms will we use to resolve disputes?

— What should be our policy regarding dividends and share redemption?

— How will we assure that minority shareholders are heard and are treated fairly?

— Under what conditions would we sell the business?

— Where will accountability lie—with an outside board of directors or with the family shareholder group?

No matter what an ownership configuration looks like, the business and family benefit when shareholding siblings form a smoothly functioning team. And when they do so, they set a positive example for the succeeding cousin generation, when ownership becomes even more diverse and complex.

**EXHIBIT 8**

## *5 Signs of Good Owners*

— See themselves as stewards of the business.

— Consider the welfare of others—the business, the family, and other shareholders—as well as their own.

— Educate themselves about business ownership.

— Understand that ownership is a privilege.

— Try to add value to the business as an institution.

*Family Business Ownership: How To Be an Effective Shareholder* by Craig E. Aronoff, Ph.D and John L. Ward, Ph.D.

# VIII. *The Evolving Roles of Leader and Successor*

## Leadership Transitions: The Good, the Bad and the Ugly

There may be five common ways for a family business leader to leave a company in the hands of successor. Each represents one model of the transition of management control from a CEO to a successor, and we have our own special names for them:

1. Cold Turkey

2. Delay and Delay and...

3. Here, Gone, Here, Gone...

4. Gradual/Progressive

5. Non-family CEO

The following illustrations demonstrate how each model works. From your reading of this booklet and from your own life experience, you will no doubt recognize each type.

### 1. Cold Turkey

The CEO maintains control until death, an accident, or illness forces a sudden departure requiring the successor to assume control immediately without the benefit of preparation.

**EXHIBIT 9** ■■■■■■■■■■■■■■■■■■■■■■■■■■■■■■■

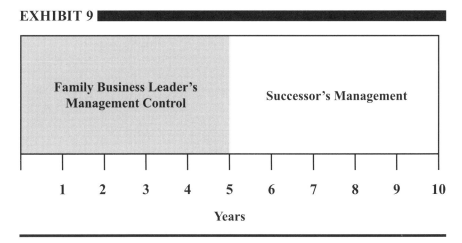

| Family Business Leader's Management Control | Successor's Management |

1    2    3    4    5    6    7    8    9    10

**Years**

**Cold Turkey Advantages:**

- Succession does occur.

- The family does not have to endure the conflict so typical of the transition phase, when the leader is letting go and the successor is acquiring more responsibilities.

**Cold Turkey Disadvantages:**

- Suddenly thrust into leadership, successors may fail, as there is no chance to acquire experience with lesser amounts of responsibility before the business' success becomes dependent upon them.

**2. Delay and Delay and...**

The CEO retains control yet keeps promising a transition. At points, some control is transferred to the successor. However, while a promise of full transfer of control is made, it is delayed and delayed.

**EXHIBIT 10**

Successor's Management Control

Family Business Leader's Management Control

1    2    3    4    5    6    7    8    9    10

**Years**

**Delay and Delay...Disadvantages:**

- The successor may get frustrated and leave.

- The successor learns to be a good follower instead of a leader, and he or she may plan to retire before the parent does, leaving the business without a successor.

- The business may decline as a result of the leader's unwillingness to adopt new strategies or invest in strategic opportunities that carry even moderate risk.

## 3. Here, Gone, Here, Gone...

The leader turns over control very quickly and then goes on a long trip, retreats to a seasonal residence, or a takes a sabbatical to become deeply involved in a passionate interest. Then, he reappears, changing many initiatives introduced in his absence and re-assuming control, often without changing titles.

**EXHIBIT 11**

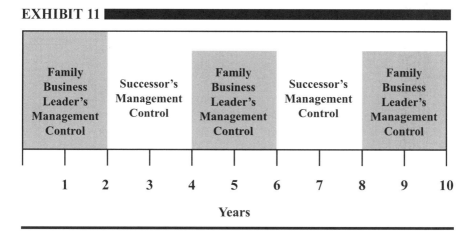

### Here, Gone, Here, Gone...Advantages:

• Succession does occur, for a while, and the successor gains experience.

### Here, Gone, Here, Gone...Disadvantages:

• The successor may get frustrated and leave.

• Pulled in two directions, placed in the middle of conflict, and seeing the initiatives they implemented under the successor undermined or removed by the reappearing leader, key employees get frustrated and leave.

## 4. Gradual/Progressive

The family business leader gradually cedes more and more responsibility to the successor, and at some point between year 5 and 6, no one notices that a transition in effective control has shifted to the successor. By year 10, the successor is fully in charge.

45

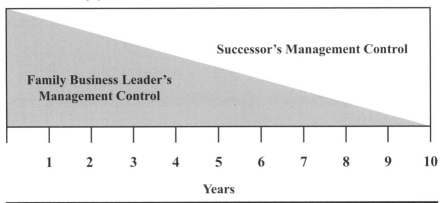

**EXHIBIT 12(A)**

Successor's Management Control

Family Business Leader's
Management Control

1   2   3   4   5   6   7   8   9   10

Years

Or, the family business leader does not make a complete transition out of the firm. Instead, he or she assumes a contributing and rewarding role, remaining available for guidance.

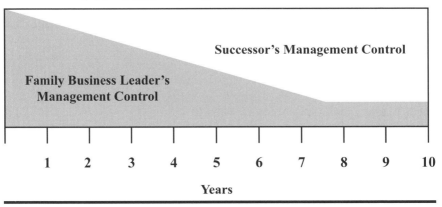

**EXHIBIT 12(B)**

Successor's Management Control

Family Business Leader's
Management Control

1   2   3   4   5   6   7   8   9   10

Years

### Gradual/Progressive Advantages:

- The successor gains experience gradually, using the time to absorb the lessons of leadership.

- With fewer responsibilities, the leader can use the transition period to explore options for the next stage of life.

### Gradual/Progressive Disadvantages:

- There is more opportunity for tension. As authority is handed off one duty at a time, there may be differences over how the successor manages each new responsibility. And as the younger generation eagerly seeks more leadership responsibility, the incumbent may react as if he or she is being pushed out.

46

## 5. Non-Family CEO

In this scenario, the family business leader transfers control to a non-family CEO (who assumes effective control at year 2), while the family business leader gradually withdraws from the firm, completing the transition by year 4. Then, the non-family CEO begins to mentor the family successor, who assumes control on the retirement of the non-family CEO at year 7.

**EXHIBIT 13**

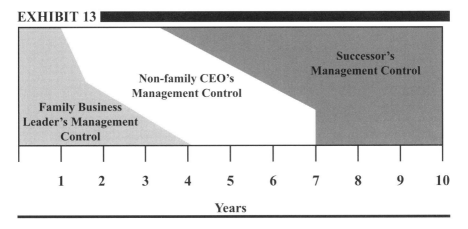

### Non-family CEO Advantages:

- When successors are not yet ready, an interim non-family CEO can be very effective in developing the skills of the next family leader.

- A respected non-family leader can introduce new skill sets to the business and implement needed innovations and changes more easily than a family successor trying to do the same thing.

### Non-family CEO Disadvantages:

- It may be difficult to find and recruit an individual with all of the needed qualifications.

The fifth option, Non-Family CEO, works well provided the right individual can be found to fill the interim leadership slot and understands the role to be played. In addition, family members must be clear about the reasons for using this form of transition.

The Cold Turkey model offers too bumpy a ride and opens the door wide to business failure. The Delay and the Here, Gone options tend to result in resentment within the family and confusion within the business, as well as stagnation of the business and a failure to develop future leadership.

It probably comes as no surprise that we have a bias toward the fourth model,

Gradual/Progressive. In our experience, it promises the greatest assurances for a smooth, successful transition. It provides the best safeguards for protecting the health of the family and the capacity of the business to thrive. And it offers the widest and most creative opportunities for the successor to develop into a solid leader and for the outgoing CEO to plan and implement an active, satisfying life on retirement.

No athlete, no matter how swift or skilled, would enter a relay race without first practicing the transfer of the baton. Step by step, the runner learns the graceful exchange needed to accept the responsibility of team leadership from another.

The same is true of the family-business successor. Once designated, he or she must practice the skills of leadership. By the time the founder and successor pass the baton, they complete the transfer at full speed. The result: a continuity that sustains the team's overall momentum while bringing new energy and power to the race.

Much is at stake. If the handoff goes poorly, with one runner clinging to the baton or the other fumbling it, the race is lost. A successor may resign or be dismissed, casting a shadow on the family and the future of the business.

Many family businesses make a mistake at this stage. Often, the heir apparent is given a broad title such as executive vice president, asked to learn as much as possible about the business, and left to drift without assuming authority over anything. Then at his or her "coronation," all the responsibility suddenly is handed over, and the successor is expected to begin running at full speed.

**A better method is to give the successor new responsibilities one by one,** in a phased transition that is clear to everyone involved. Five years before the successor takes control of operations as president, he or she might be given responsibility for sales and marketing. Two years later, production or operations is added. In another year, the successor may take on finance and administration.

Ideally, the incumbent CEO is less and less involved in decision-making during this period. Early in the process, each of the successor's decisions may require parental involvement and approval. Next, the parent may be asked for concurrence after a decision has been made. Then the parent is only informed of decisions after the fact. Finally, the successor seeks the parent's counsel only when needed, as though the incumbent were a consultant on call.

One successor describes this period as a process of "finding inner confidence." The first year after he assumed the role of general manager, he recalls, "I'd call Dad almost daily to ask him about just about everything." By the second year, he picked up the phone only on Tuesdays and Thursdays. "If my father was out, he'd always get back to me by the next day."

By the third year, "I'd call on Tuesdays, and he'd call back sometimes a week later. Sometimes I'd just forget to call him on some things. By then, we realized that the transition was complete."

Important business relationships need to be transferred to the new leader, too. The CEO should at some point list key people—advisors, suppliers, customers, bankers, and others—and introduce each to the successor so that new relationships can be formed.

## Taking the Helm

When the successor finally becomes CEO, he or she should be given broad authority for all areas not specifically assigned to the predecessor, who typically becomes chairman.

**The chairman keeps responsibility only for a list of clearly defined functions** traditionally reserved for the board: dividends, approving a capital budget, debt levels, acquisitions and divestitures, and hiring, firing, and compensation of officers.

This retains the parent's control over such sensitive decisions as firing a veteran manager, setting family members' salaries, or selling key operations. But it gives management freedom to the successor, who needs latitude at this stage to begin running the business and meeting strategic goals in his or her own way.

**Clear job descriptions for both the successor and the founder at all stages are crucial** in staying the course and preventing misunderstandings and mistrust among employees.

Finally, the transition has to end. The founder must surrender authority, preferably by an agreed-upon date. Usually, the transfer of ownership control follows.

## Letting Go Gracefully

Few statements irritate a successor more than a parent's saying, "I'm retired—more or less." As one son put it: "I don't know when he's retired more and when he's retired less."

But outgoing leaders often like the "more or less" concept. They can lead a life of leisure when they feel like it. They can drop in on the business and "straighten things out" when they feel like it, too. They have the best of both worlds.

But all the while, the successor may be biting his or her lip to contain anger. The successor is eager to lead the business. But how is he or she to know whether the founder is more or less in control at any given time? How would you feel as CEO if your authority were open to question at any time, without notice?

"One of my strategies has been to just get out of the way," said one business owner after turning the leadership of his industrial boiler manufacturing company over to his two sons. "I remember back when I was their age and how I thought about my dad—that if he'd just get out of the way! So, I tried to put that into practice."

His sons expressed great admiration for their father. "I think it's quite a testament to Dad that he's allowing us to do what we want to do, and not what he wants us to do," said one.

Consider again the relay race we described at the beginning of this chapter. Imagine the consequences if the runner passing the baton doesn't get out of the way: a stumble or a collision, a dropped baton, or even possibly permanent injury to the athletes.

And if the baton is passed too late, all is lost—including the race. In one family business, a 91-year-old founder delegated check-signing authority to his 64-year-old son only because his hand was shaking too badly to write. In another, a

*Owners need to establish a firm deadline for transferring power.* third-generation manager at 58 was eagerly anticipating retirement—well before his 79-year-old father had even thought of it. Such malingering elders waste potential, not only of the younger generation but also probably of the business itself.

Owners need to establish a firm deadline for transferring power. A board of outside directors or advisors can help them stick to the schedule.

As successors gradually assume more authority, parents can begin new activities just as gradually. Most entrepreneurs find the need more than just recreation and leisure—as we discussed at length in Chapter III, they need responsibility for leadership and development of something new. They can use the transition period to explore new options for themselves and determine how they will use their lives once the succession is complete.

Above all, the outgoing leader should avoid returning to the business after the leadership transition is accomplished. Many entrepreneurs are tempted to do this two to five years after retirement, especially if they retain voting stock control. Such a move may seriously damage family relationships, and the presence of two "leaders" can have a devastating effect on the business as well. **The founder should strongly consider relinquishing voting stock control at the time of retirement-if not before.**

### A Personal Rationale for the Outgoing CEO

The transfer zone in leadership succession is often particularly painful. The process requires trust between the leader and the successor. Both must be committed to success. The parent must be enthusiastic about passing on the business, and the successor must be deserving of authority.

Even with all these ingredients present, the parent may go through a grieving period. The son or daughter may also suffer pain, perhaps because of disagreements over power, money, or the successor's readiness to do the job.

Just as the successor needs a personal rationale, the CEO must think through what makes succession so worthwhile. "It's difficult now, but it's worth it because... ," the leader may say, filling in the blanks with any number of important reasons—from "we employ a lot of people; my daughter will make this company grow and employ even more" to "I'm proud to have created an organization that can survive."

Sorting out your feelings will help you through this difficult time. Outside directors, trusted professional advisors, or other peers can act as a catalyst, conscience, or source of personal support in the letting-go process.

# IX. *Implementing Succession*

A succession process isn't complete until the transition from one leader to the next has actually taken place. How a family business "gets from here to there" requires forethought, tact, and the ability to ease the fears of those affected by the change of leadership. And both outgoing CEO and successor will have to be deeply involved during this stage of the process.

### Communicating the Decision

The way the succession decision is communicated to the family and the company can have an enormous impact on the outcome. If other family members or key managers think that one candidate was pulled out of the pack just because he or she was Mom or Dad's favorite, that successor will lack credibility and authority from the start.

On the other hand, **if it is clear to everyone involved that the successor survived a planned selection process based on objective criteria, the transition is likely to go more smoothly.** This means that communication with the family about succession should begin as soon as possible, ideally before any candidates have been identified.

Once a choice is made, the decision should be conveyed with sensitivity to the members of both family and business. As much as possible, the message should avoid leaving any family members feeling inferior to the person chosen. On the other hand, it should leave no room for doubt that the successor is capable, in control, and honored.

According to Susan E. Tifft and Alex S. Jones, in their book *The Trust: The Private and Powerful Family Behind The New York Times,* Arthur Ochs "Punch" Sulzberger was very concerned that the family view the process of selecting a fourth-generation successor as a fair one. His son, Arthur Jr., was already publisher of *The New York Times*, but Punch had two other titles to give up: chairman and CEO of the company. He knew the family would not permit all three titles to go to one person.

Punch spent much time discussing the decision with key family members and with consultants brought in to help with the process. Ultimately, with the backing of the board of directors, Arthur Jr. was named chairman of the company in addition to his role as publisher of the *Times*; a highly respected non-family executive was named CEO; and Punch's nephew, Michael Golden, young Arthur's chief rival, was appointed vice chairman—a plan the family accepted.

Before the plan was announced, however, Punch spent several weeks not only telling his co-owning sisters about it, but also visiting

*Communication with the family about succession should begin as soon as possible, ideally before any candidates have been identified.*

51

each of his directors and phoning each of the cousins in the next generation. There were some predictably hurt feelings among some of the 13 cousins. But they, like their parents and the entire cousin group, saw themselves as stewards of the company and especially of the cherished *New York Times*, and their commitment helped them, in time, to move past their personal disappointment.

Most family businesses say too little about the succession decision for fear of offending someone. The result is that no one assigns much importance to the shift in authority. This can undermine the successor.

Once succession plans are firm, the CEO should make clear publicly that he or she intends to retire. The company's mission, strategy, and values should be expressed at the same time, along with key elements of the succession plan.

When the transition takes place, the CEO and successor should prepare a joint statement to the company that articulates again the business's objectives and strategy and describes all shifts in responsibility. Some statement about the outgoing leader's post-retirement plans should be part of this announcement, particularly if he or she continues to play any role in relation to the business. This leaves no room for confusion or, worse, for the return of the departing CEO. Successors face a special communications challenge. In the unique world of family business, each new generation of management needs to rediscover for itself the meaning of ownership and leadership and to find new ways to articulate it.

Successors should try above all to communicate commitment to the enterprise and to the family. They need not—and should not—pretend to be just like the predecessor. But they can make great strides toward effective leadership by expressing similar passion and enthusiasm for the business in their own distinct way.

When Steve Forbes, successor to Malcolm Forbes as head of the Forbes publishing empire, took over after his father's death, he didn't pretend to become his flamboyant predecessor.

"Many have asked... aren't you worried that the firm will be hurt by the fact that you seem to lack your father's attention-getting style?"

Steve Forbes wrote in his inaugural *Forbes* issue as chief executive.

"Pop would be very disappointed if I tried to imitate him," Steve continued. "'I have my own way of doing things, and, in time, you will develop yours,' he told me more than 20 years ago. 'Don't try to be what you're not.'"

"So while styles may change, the spirit that animates this magazine and our other enterprises will remain

> *Once succession plans are firm, the CEO should make clear publicly that he or she intends to retire. The company's mission, strategy, and values should be expressed at the same time, along with key elements of the succession plan.*

*Once the leadership transition is complete, an era passes for both founder and successor and some sadness may ensue. But for the family and the business, the transfer is a new milestone on the path to continuity.*

constant. My father and I shared a similarly intense love for this business."

Steve added, "there is no replacing my father, but I bring the same spirit of dedication and joy to the job that he did..."

Perhaps most important, **the effective successor sees stewardship of the family's assets as a privilege and takes care to communicate that attitude to others.** For many years, Malcolm Forbes had told family members that he intended to give Steve both management and ownership control. "As one said to me, 'Don't blow our inheritance.' In my interest and theirs—I will work to increase it," Steve wrote.

Once the leadership transition is complete, an era passes for both founder and successor and some sadness may ensue. But for the family and the business, the transfer is a new milestone on the path to continuity.

### Succession Is Holistic

Family business owners often think of succession planning only in terms of the business's leadership.

But **succession brings profound change to the entire organization and to the family as a whole.** New career paths for other key executives, changes in the corporate culture, new management systems and styles—all can bring tremendous stress. Briefly, here are some critical aspects of implementing organizational succession.

**—The Management Team.** A new management team must be developed in a way that will support the successor, but it's a process that requires careful handling. The succession plan should describe the successor's opportunities to make changes in top management—an area that can be especially sensitive for the departing CEO. Will longtime loyal executives be retained? Are any positions redundant with those held by the successor's chosen team? These questions can stir competitive feelings between parents and offspring.

However painful it may be to an outgoing leader and to key executives who may be moved to other positions or asked to retire or leave, successors eventually deserve their own management teams. As long as the successor is working with the predecessor's team, he or she may feel like a junior partner. The process of creating her own executive team "has been one of very much coming into my own," Julia H. Klein, president and CEO of C.H. Briggs Hardware Company, a distributor in Reading, Pa., once told *Nation's Business* magazine.

The successor should choose a team that meets the business' strategic needs. At the same time, the predecessor's managers need the successor's respect. "There's a huge balancing act for me between honoring somebody's past contribution and building for the future," Klein said. But she found that some of the managers she inherited weren't the best fit for future. She treated them "with as much dignity and respect as I could," and provided them with a generous severance.

**EXHIBIT 14** ▉▉▉▉▉▉▉▉▉▉▉▉▉▉▉▉▉▉▉▉▉▉▉▉▉▉▉▉▉▉▉

## *5 Tips for Building a Successor's Executive Team*

1. Select individuals who can meet the company's strategic needs.

2. Look for people who have skills that you don't have.

3. Develop a team that supports your leadership style.

4. Include some topnotch people from outside the company—they will raise the level of professionalism in your business.

5. Choose people who energize you and aren't afraid to challenge you.

---

**—Other Important Family and Non-Family Employees.** Just as the successor's career path has been well defined, other family members' opportunities should be charted, too. Siblings or cousins need a clear, planned course of development under the new CEO.

Career, compensation, and performance-review plans should be laid for key family and non-family managers who were not chosen as successors. A participation or employment policy for family members in the business, covering rules for entry into the company, part-time work, the role of in-laws, and so on, should be made clear.

Some companies include in their succession plans a set of rules governing family members' working relationships. One company stipulated that family members should not report to one another. It also encouraged family members to develop their own self-identity by avoiding following each other in job progressions.

**—The Board of Directors.** The makeup of the board may need to be altered to meet the needs of the new CEO. This, too, should be discussed in the succession plan and with the individuals involved, to avoid misunderstandings or hard feelings. The transition can be used as an opportunity to retire older family directors and make way for talented, younger family members. The new CEO may also want to bring in some outsiders from his or her own generation to serve as directors.

**—Accountability of the Successor.** A performance-review plan for the successor is crucial. The new CEO needs feedback, and shareholders need to know that he or she will be held accountable. The successor, after all, has a fiduciary responsibility to the business's owners.

A number of mechanisms can be used to assure accountability. An outside board of directors is particularly useful in this respect. So are family forums and shareholder meetings.

**—Shareholder Relations.** Communicating with and educating shareholders becomes more important as ownership expands to more family members in succeeding generations. The successor may take this responsibility or see to it that it is assumed by another family member.

Some family businesses embrace policies guiding shareholder communications. Here is an excerpt from one company's statement:

> "It's important that the entire family be aware of general expectations, succession plans, and arrangements with individual family members. Compensation, benefits, and perquisites are best an open book.

> "It's also important that inactive shareholders understand the demanding requirements and burdens of leadership. These are most usually under-appreciated. Career planning may seem like a special privilege, but it is essential for the strength of the business and common to all well-run companies. Informal discussions between the Board and the shareholders can clarify any questions or misunderstandings."

A leadership transition also means a time to **develop new buy-sell agreements between shareholders and new estate plans**. Any existing agreements probably cover transactions between the CEO and the company to protect the leader's spouse in the event of the CEO's death. Now, the next generation of owners, usually co-owning siblings or cousins, needs agreements that suit the new ownership structure.

**—The Family Leader.** A CEO's retirement often creates a need for a new family leader—someone who focuses on the family as family. Such an individual nurtures family traditions, looks to the family's emotional needs, sees to the education of in-laws, and keeps communication going. In the first generation, if the founder is a male, family leadership often falls to the wife.

But anyone can be the family leader—an uncle, an aunt, a grandparent and even a committee. What counts is that whoever assumes this responsibility has both heart and ability. Many successful business-owning families believe family leadership is just as important as business leadership.

A shift at the top of a family business has a domino effect that necessitates all kinds of changes in both family and business. When CEOs and their successors exhibit wisdom and care in the way these changes are handled, they minimize bruised feelings and poise both the family and the business for exciting new challenges.

# X. *Understanding Family Tensions*

Planning and implementing succession is a delicate task that breeds conflict. It can be frustrating for everyone involved.

**Many families make the mistake of assuming that all members share the same values.** In fact, siblings may have sharply different value systems. Birth order can have a big impact. So can birth dates. A firstborn might be raised by hard-pressed parents who are working night and day. By the time the fourth offspring reaches childhood, the same parents may be affluent and have a completely different lifestyle. Where the older children were expected to help out in the business, younger siblings may enjoy fewer responsibilities and more privileges. So even though siblings have grown up in the same family, they may approach life as if they had been raised by a different set of parents.

Rivalry among siblings often intensifies in the family business. While competition can motivate siblings to turn in excellent job performances, it can also careen out of control, sparking divisive battles that hurt the company.

Whether they like it or not, family-business siblings also find themselves harnessed with the brothers and sisters in the most fragile of business relationships—the partnership. If partnerships tend to sink friendships, imagine their impact on sibling relationships!

Children's spouses introduce another source of conflict. Spouses often don't know the family business well. When their husbands and wives return home each night, spouses may hear only about the problems at work, not the joys. Also, spouses may grow jealous over seeming inequities in family members' pay and perks. As a result, even innocent in-laws may over time tend to pull the family apart.

Role conflict is another cause of strain. Siblings easily grow to resent playing professional roles in relation to each other. "I hate to demand deadlines from my brother or ask embarrassing questions in staff meetings," one brother might say. "I can manage him, but I hate to go through that." The other brother likely has a different view: "why do I have to report back to my brother? Doesn't he trust me to know that I got the job done?"

We have also already mentioned the tension that occurs between the incumbent CEO and the successor during the transition period. The successor's growth in experience, confidence, and vision for the firm will naturally impose upon the domain of the CEO. The CEO may feel that he or she is being pushed out. Or the CEO may disagree with the successor's strategy, leadership style or choice of executive hires.

And there may be tension at home. The wife of a newly retired CEO will resent it if her husband, with time on his hands, starts to tell her how to run the household.

**Whatever the problem, you're not alone; thousands of other business-owning families are having similar experiences.** An outside board or professional advisor can often be helpful in defusing conflict. Many families attend programs on family business as a group so they can learn together what challenges to expect during succession. Some get help from seminars on communication. One family we know consulted a family therapist to help its members resolve some of the conflicts they were experiencing.

Sometimes, getting along goes back to the basic rules of childhood. When the members of one four-sibling partnership were asked why the business relationship had worked so well, they had a short answer: "our parents taught us to trust each other."

**A little empathy for other family members can leaven difficult moments.** No matter how frustrating the children's role in succession parents also have a difficult job. How can they make a choice among children they love equally? How can they reconcile their role as discriminating managers with their role as parents who value and love their children unconditionally? When are they to act like parents, and when like managers?

Clearly, succession can be a minefield of tension and conflict for family members. It helps to know that tension is a predictable part of succession, however, and that there are more resources available than ever before to help businessowning families through troubled waters.

**EXHIBIT 15** ■■■■■■■■■■■■■■■■■■■■■■■■■■■■■■■■■

## *8 Ways To Minimize Family Tension*

— Develop empathy for one another.

— Work on communication skills, especially listening.

— Give top priority to the best interests of the business.

— Spend some time away from each other.

— But also spend time with each other just for fun, with no business talk allowed.

— Develop a family code of conduct outlining how family members will treat one another.

— Educate in-laws about the business and how it works.

— Don't be afraid to seek outside help.

# XI. *Other Pitfalls: Where Are You Most Likely to Stumble?*

Some pitfalls of succession have already been mentioned. But a few are so common that they deserve as closer look:

**—No Safety Net.** An Achilles heel frequently found in even the most polished succession campaigns is the failure to plan for Mom and Dad's personal financial security in retirement.

Before they can give up control gracefully, parents need to know that their future is financially solid (preferably independent of the business) and that their estate plans are in order. And successors need to know that this parental well being can't be jeopardized by any management risk that they may take.

Once succession is complete, **parents should be able to sustain their standard of living indefinitely without relying on their children or the business.** Without this security net, a destructive dynamic can develop that saps the momentum of the business: Parents may worry that their kids take too many risks in managing the business. And the children may grow increasingly risk-averse because they're worried about their parents' financial security. The business can stagnate or lack entrepreneurship.

As this dynamic shows, succession planning in the family business is like an equation. A family can't complete a good succession plan unless the parents' estate and personal financial plans are in place. Estate planning can't be conducted without succession plans for management and ownership. And, as mentioned earlier, two other key plans—a family statement of mission and a strategic plan—are crucial to this equation, too.

**—Setting the Kids Up To Fail.** Some founders, in an unconscious attempt to prove they are indispensable, actually sabotage their successors without realizing it.

"This business is nothing without me," one founder said as he prepared to retire and hand control over to his son. "It takes a lot of capital to operate it. But there's no way I would leave enough money in the company for my son to run it, because he'd just blow it."

One problem was that the father didn't trust his son. But a deeper impulse was to prove that he was essential. He wanted to have the last word ("I told you it would never work without me!") and, in a perverse way, to prolong his presence in the business even after he had retired.

In his own negative way, this founder is trying to achieve immortality. But the result will be destructive for everyone concerned.

**—Shareholder Conflict.** Another pitfall is the potential for conflict between passive shareholders and those who are active in the business.

As the business passes to the second and especially the third and fourth generations of family ownership, the interests of these two groups diverge. **Passive shareholders may begin to see the business as a birthright,** and they may resent the pay and perks of family members who are working in the business. Also, active shareholders may resent the demands of passive owners for dividends and liquidity.

This problem is worsened by the fact that the small to medium-sized family business must grow very fast to support multiple offspring in the same style as their parents. Resentments over having to settle for dwindling shares of the same pie can flare into destructive family clashes that drain the business.

In large businesses with many family shareholders, these problems can often be managed as if it were a public company. Shareholder meetings and the formation of a family council become vehicles for finding consensus and defining the proper role of passive owners.

But in family businesses with only a few shareholders, ownership and management often is kept in the same hands. This approach requires some work on writing buy-sell agreements and securing cash to buyout passive owners. But it can pay big dividends in the form of peaceful growth for the business.

—**Parental Impasse.** Sometimes family business CEOs simply find it too difficult to address important aspects of succession planning and implementation. This may leave the successor stalled, wondering, "how am I ever going to get anything going around here?"

Sometimes, peers of the parent can help him or her face the need. A successor might turn to a respected lawyer, accountant, or other advisor with a secure relationship with the CEO and say, "I don't want to sound too pushy, but isn't it unusual that we have no stock-transfer plan? Could you talk to my father about this?" The trusted peer may be able to bring up the issue in a way the CEO can tolerate.

Family members, however, usually shouldn't be used just as sounding boards, however. Venting one's frustration on Mom or another family member in hopes of finding an ally only creates triangles that can block a constructive, peaceful solution.

# XII. *Summary*

**Preparing to pass the family business on to the next generation is perhaps the toughest and most critical challenge facing the business owner.** But the succession process also poses a unique opportunity to perpetuate the privileges and rewards of private business ownership.

It's the responsibility of the incumbent CEO to initiate and manage the succession process and to do it in a timely fashion. One of the most important steps is the earliest one: inculcating cherished values and a sense of stewardship in one's children while they are still small.

But the process begins in earnest about 15 years before the actual transition is to occur. CEOs have a lot of work to do during this period: getting estate plans and a strategic business plan in order; laying out a fair process for identifying and choosing successors; training potential successors. A CEO must also prepare the family for succession, a task that includes the development of a family mission statement that articulates the family's commitment to the business. Beginning as early as they can understand, the children also need to be educated for their future role as owners, and must be schooled to function as a team, whether or not they work in the business. And, the CEO must also prepare the business itself, making sure that the successor is heir to a company that is in excellent health.

Once a potential successor or successors have been developed and a choice has been made, leadership and ownership control of the business should be transferred in a step-by-step process that allows both founder and successor to assume their new roles smoothly and with a minimum of pain and disruption. Finally, the incumbent leader should devote time and thought to preparing for a financially secure and enjoyable retirement, plotting activities that will be at least as creative and exciting as those he or she has left behind.

Succession in a family firm is everybody's business. Everyone in the company and everyone in the family is going to be affected somehow—parents, children, grandchildren, shareholders, family executives, non-family executives, employees, the board of directors, and even suppliers and customers. Those most directly involved will have fears and concerns about their future and need to be treated with respect and sensitivity by the outgoing CEO and the successor.

There will be some tension during the succession process and an occasional conflict may erupt. But wise business families understand that stress and disagreements are a predictable part of the transition. They know that empathy for one another can help prevent and heal rifts. And when a situation threatens to get out of hand, they are quick to seek professional help.

Succession is often the most painful stage in the life cycle of the family business. **Yet many owners take pride, and rightly so, in creating or preserving an institution that can outlast them. They find great reward in assuring the continuity of an organization that will foster a strong family identity and perpetuate the family's values, goals, and well being in the next generation and perhaps for generations to come.**

# Further References:

**Books**

*Creating Effective Boards for Private Enterprises: Meeting the Challenges of Continuity and Competition* by John L. Ward, Ph.D. ©2001 Family Enterprise Publishers.

*Developing Family Business Policies: Your Guide to the Future* by Craig E. Aronoff, Ph.D., Joseph H. Astrachan, Ph.D. and John L. Ward, Ph.D. ©1998 Family Enterprise Publishers.

*Family Business Governance: Maximizing Family and Business Potential,* Craig E. Aronoff, Ph.D. and John L. Ward, Ph.D. ©1996 Family Enterprise Publishers.

*Family Business Ownership: How To Be an Effective Shareholder* by Craig E. Aronoff, Ph.D. and John L. Ward, Ph.D. ©2001 Family Enterprise Publishers.

*Family Meetings: How To Build a Stronger Family and a Stronger Business 2nd edition* by Craig E. Aronoff, Ph.D. and John L. Ward, Ph.D. ©2002 Family Enterprise Publishers.

*Making Sibling Teams Work: The Next Generation* by Craig E. Aronoff, Ph.D., Joseph H. Astrachan, Ph.D., Drew S. Mendoza and John L. Ward, Ph.D. ©1997 Family Enterprise Publishers.

*The Trust: The Private and Power Family Behind The New York Times* by Susan E. Tifft and Alex S. Jones. ©1999 Little, Brown & Company.

**Articles**

*A Message from Forbes' President: The Spirit Remains* by Malcolm S. Forbes, Jr. Reprinted from *Forbes Magazine* in *Family Business Sourcebook II.* ©1990 Forbes Inc.

*Don't Choose Your Own Successor* by Harry Levinson. *Harvard Business Review,* November/December 1974. ©1974 by the President and Fellows of Harvard College.

*Healthy Motivations for Family Business Succession* by Carl "Terry" Plochman, III. *The Family Business Advisor,* January 1998. ©1998 Family Enterprise Publishers.

*Pre-Mortem Beats Post-Mortem* by Craig E. Aronoff, Ph.D. *The Family Business Advisor,* April 2002. ©2002 Family Enterprise Publishers.

# *Appendix A*
# *One Family's Emergency Succession Plan Example*

The following plan was developed for the unlikely event of a tragedy involving the CEO, which would render him unavailable. The sequence of steps would be as follows:

1. At a family meeting, initial steps will be discussed and the question will be answered, "Given the nature of the business and the family, and the experience of our current Board members, are additional advisors needed?" If so, they will be identified and added to the Advisory Board immediately. The Advisory Board will have, as its primary purpose, the responsibility of advising the family throughout the crisis.

2. A Board meeting will be called which will include all adult members of the family. The main agenda items will be a plan for the business, roles of family members during the crisis, and communications among the family. A decision on an overall direction (emergency strategy) will be made at this meeting.

3. A second Board meeting will be held, this time including just the family shareholders, to develop a more specific plan of action. However, the Board may request the counsel of others in the organization, such as the Chief Operating Officer or Chief Financial Officer. Topics of focus will include:

   a. Board of Director issues, i.e., membership and actions they must take

   b. Shareholder actions required, if any

   c. Leadership in key positions within the company

   d. Damage control with key customers, suppliers, and/or other outsiders

   e. On-going affairs and business of the organization

4. A shareholders' meeting will be called if needed, during which there will be decisions regarding follow through on the recommendations of the Board. The Board of Directors will appoint management and monitor management's compliance with directives and emergency succession follow through actions within the firm.

# *Appendix B*
# *Family Council Charter Example*

## Origin

At our Family Business Retreat on October 7, 20xx, it was decided that a Family Council will be formed involving all family members age 16 or above. The purpose of the Council will be to educate and facilitate communication among family members, and to provide a forum for constructive discussion, problem-solving, and decisions about the family as it relates to Smith Company as well as the business as it relates to the family.

## Purpose of the Family Council

Two immediate, short-term purposes for the Council are to provide a forum for:

1. Managing the transition from John and Mary Smith's generation to the next; and

2. Building teamwork among the next generation of owners of Smith Company.

In addition to these initial purposes are other objectives that we will strive to accomplish:

1. We want a forum for constructive discussion to deal with the known and unknown challenges that confront us as a family in business together. Our intention is to deal with challenges directly and the Family Council will be the forum for doing so.

2. We expect the Council, as an informal body, to afford regular contact among family members and to be used to nurture relationships among members of the extended family and between current owners and the next generation of owners.

3. The Council will provide a place for general communication among family members involved in the business. It is a place for questions to get answered and for all of us to learn what each other thinks about issues that affect us all. Our intention is to encourage and to make it "okay" for family members to bring up issues and have them addressed properly.

4. As we go forward, we will need to learn. The Council will provide an

opportunity for individuals with special expertise to address us and help educate us about issues affecting our family relations, investments, or the business.

5. The Council will be a place for decision making. We will benefit by having a forum where all members have a voice in decisions that affect them. Our Council will provide that opportunity.

6. And finally, for decisions that directly impact the business, the Council will serve as the family's voice and provide its input directly to the Board of Directors. Therefore, for issues on which the Board needs guidance from its shareholders, the Council will serve as a forum for family decision making and consensus on the direction that is provided to the Board. The Family Council will not limit direct communication between any shareholder and the Corporation, but, instead, will serve as an additional conduit for communication between the family and its legal representatives to the Corporation, the Board of Directors.

# Organization of the Family Council

### Meeting Structure
Meetings will be held off-site, meaning away from the business. A setting where we can meet without interruptions will be selected and arranged for by the host (the family member who organizes a particular meeting).

Each Council meeting will have two phases. Phase One will be a meeting of the next generation of shareholders. Phase Two will include all shareholders and other family members. In general, the first phase of the meeting will be for the business of the next generation, and the second will be for the business of the family as a whole.

### Frequency of Meetings
For the first year, meetings will be held monthly. Thereafter, meetings will be held as needed, but no less than quarterly.

### Membership
All stockholding lineal descendants of John and Mary Smith, their spouses, and their children age 16 and above are members of the Family Council.

# Appendix C
# Forging Your Family Mission

Members of a business-owning family can use the following questions as a guide to discussions that will help them clarify the family's mission for the business.

## Our Values

1. As a family, what beliefs do we hold in common? What are the values behind each of our beliefs?

2. What business practice(s) would be so abhorrent to us that we would sooner choose not be in business before we would conduct ourselves in such a way? What values would be violated?

## Purpose of the Business

1. Why continue the business as a family owned enterprise?

2. When, or under what circumstances, might we decide we want to sell the business?

3. What unique purpose is being served through our ownership of the business that would be lost if we were no longer a private company?

## The Family's Vision of the Future

Business vision is a critical element of a business' success and should be developed with significant involvement of company management. Fundamental to a shared business and family vision, is the family's vision for the future.

1. What qualifications must family members have for positions in the business?

2. What philosophy should be followed for making compensation decisions for family members?

3. What qualifications will apply for leadership of the business?

4. What style of management (culture) does the family prefer and want to promote?

5. To what degree is our ownership of the business an investment and to what degree is it a stewardship responsibility?

6. Who qualifies for a board position?

7. How do we protect the contributions of good, non-family employees?

8. What responsibility do we have to our communities?

9. What strengths (advantages) do we expect the family to contribute to the business?

10. What is our position on business risk?

11. What is our position on our image in the marketplace?

12. How will objectivity be introduced into decisions regarding family member positions jobs, leadership roles, compensation, governance roles)?

## Mission

The mission, oversimplified, is to accomplish the vision and remain consistent with our values and purpose. A more suitable mission statement would fall from the answers to the above questions and be consistent with the family's and firm's cultures.

# *Index*

# The Authors

**Craig E. Aronoff, Ph.D.**

Co-founder and principal of The Family Business Consulting Group, Inc., Craig Aronoff is a leading consultant, speaker, writer, and educator in the family business field.

As the founder of the Cox Family Enterprise Center at Kennesaw State University in Marietta, GA, Aronoff invented and implemented the membership-based, professional-service-provider sponsored Family Business Forum, which has served as a model of family business education for some 150 universities world-wide. Until his retirement, he held the Dinos Eminent Scholar Distinguished Chair of Private Enterprise and is currently professor emeritus of management in Kennesaw State's Coles College of Business.

As a consultant, Aronoff has worked with hundreds of family companies in the U.S. and abroad on issues including generational transitions; developing business and family governance processes and structures; finding and articulating family missions and values; facilitating decision making and conflict resolution; managerial development; family compensation and dividend policies; family meetings; and more. As an inspiring, informative and entertaining speaker on a variety of family business topics, he speaks regularly to trade and professional groups and has lectured at over 80 universities.

With co-author John L. Ward, Aronoff is perhaps the most prolific writer in the family business field. He has authored, co-authored or been editor of more than two dozen books, including the multi-volume Family Business Leadership Series and is executive editor of *The Family Business Advisor.*

Listed in Who's Who and widely acknowledged for his work in the area of family business, Aronoff has received, among other honors: the Family Firm Institute's Beckhard Award for Outstanding Contributions to Family Business Practice; The Freedom Foundation's Leavey Award for Excellence in Private Enterprise Education; and the National Federation of Independent Business Foundation's Outstanding Educator Award.

Aronoff grew up in a family business. He received his bachelor's degree from Northwestern University, his Masters from the University of Pennsylvania, and his Doctorate from the University of Texas at Austin.

**Stephen L. McClure, Ph.D.**

Steve is a principal of The Family Business Consulting Group, Inc. and is an experienced facilitator and organization development consultant. He specializes in family/non-family management teamwork, governance, successor development and team development, management and leadership succession, strategic planning, and management processes tailored to family firms.

In 1999, McClure was awarded the Family Firm Institute's Beckhard Award for Outstanding Contributions to Family Business Practice. He is also a recipient of the National University Continuing Education Association's Creativity Award for developing the program, Managing in a Family Business.

Steve has been published in *Family Business Magazine, Private Wealth Management, The Family Business Client, Building Strong Family Teams Handbook, and Organization Development Annual.* McClure is also a member of the Editorial Board of the international journal, *The Family Business Client.* He has been quoted on family business issues in *Entrepreneur Magazine, Success Magazine* and *Nation's Business.* He is a regular guest lecturer at the University of Notre Dame MBA program and a keynote speaker to associations of business owners and family business forums in the United States and the United Kingdom.

He received his Ph.D. in Organizational Behavior from the Krannert Graduate School of Management at Purdue University. His undergraduate degree is in psychology.

### John L. Ward, Ph.D.

A co-founder of The Family Business Consulting Group, Inc., clinical professor at Kellogg School of Management and Wild Group Professor of Family Business at IMD, Ward teaches strategic management, business leadership and family enterprise continuity. He is an active researcher, speaker and consultant on family succession, ownership, governance and philanthropy.

He is the author of three leading texts on family business, *Keeping the Family Business Healthy, Creating Effective Boards for Private Enterprises, and, Strategic Planning for the Family Business.* He is also co-author of a collection of booklets, The Family Business Leadership Series, each focusing on specific issues family businesses face.

Ward graduated from Northwestern University (B.A.) and Stanford Graduate School of Business (M.B.A. and Ph.D.). He is the co-director of The Center for Family Enterprises at Kellogg and currently serves on the boards of several companies inthe U.S. and Europe. He conducts regular seminars in Spain, Italy, India, Hong Kong, Sweden, and Switzerland.

John and his wife, Gail, a Chicago high school principal, live in Evanston, Illinois. They have two adult children. They are active in community and educational activities and enjoy family travel and sports.